GROWING UP WILD

Alexia Barrable and Duncan Barrable

A HOW TO BOOK

ROBINSON

First published in Great Britain in 2017 by Robinson

1 3 5 7 9 10 8 6 4 2

NOTE: The material contained is for general guidance and does not deal with particular circumstances. The ideas and activities in this book are compiled from historical and modern sources and personal experience and are not intended to replace the advice of professional practitioners. The law assumes that anyone engaged in outdoor activities should take care of their own safety and that of the children in their care. The publisher cannot take any responsibility for any personal injury or damage that might result from any of the activities in this book.

A CIP catalogue record for this book
is available from the British Library.

ISBN: 978-1-47213-904-7

Typeset in Avenir LT by Hewer Text UK Ltd, Edinburgh
Printed and bound by CPI Group (UK) Ltd, Croydon, CR0 4YY

Papers used by Robinson are from well-managed forests and other responsible sources.

Robinson
An imprint of
Little, Brown Book Group
Carmelite House
50 Victoria Embankment
London EC4Y 0DZ

An Hachette UK Company
www.hachette.co.uk

www.littlebrown.co.uk

Contents

PART TWO: THE ACTIVITIES

Acknowledgements

Writing a book always takes many more people than just those who do the writing. We have been supported by many at Little, Brown, not least Nikki Read and Giles Lewis, who were enthusiastic and supportive of the idea of *Growing Up Wild* right from the start.

Another thanks goes to all the parents of children young and old(er) who shared their success and failures in all outdoor endeavours, from camping to running and from spear fishing (hint: don't do it!) to tree climbing. You, and your children, are inspiration to us all.

A big heartfelt thank you goes to our families, especially our parents, who instilled a love of all things outdoors and wild. We hope to be able to pass on the same love to our own children, and to our readers too.

Finally, this book would not even have been conceived if it weren't for our two sons, Joe and Oliver, who have helped us rediscover the natural world. Through their young eyes we have been able to look at everything with a sense of fresh wonder and playfulness. This book is for them!

Preface

As an educator I have been very excited by all the research coming from the social and medical sciences on the diverse and, it seems, very real benefits of children spending time outdoors. As a young mother, on the other hand, and as a person who grew up very much in touch with nature, it all seems a little obvious to me. In fact it was extremely early into my new role as a mum, and with an untold sense of relief no less, that I worked out the magic powers of taking a fussy baby out into the open air. Some of my most vivid memories of early motherhood lie in just those moments: the instant calm under the acacia in our garden, watching the play of light and shadow, the leaves gently moving in the breeze. In those early days of motherhood the garden, the tree, the breath of the wind all offered solace both for me and my baby.

In my first book, *Growing Up Happy,* co-written with neuroscientist Dr Jenny Barnett, one of our ten chapters on happiness and well-being in children focused on the power that the outdoors has to transform our lives and our moods, to energise and relax in equal measures, to entertain and educate. During the writing of that book, but afterwards too, I kept on looking at new research being published, at academic papers confirming what I already felt as a mum. And so, slowly, *Growing Up Wild* started taking shape in my head.

What started as a look into the mechanisms that promote our mental and physical well-being when we are in a natural environment, later became a quest for easy, exciting and diverse outdoor activities. With two young kids I found that half the time getting outside was in fact the easier option, as it helped keep my kids happy, entertained and engaged, but the other half it was a challenge: how to get ready, what to pack, where to go, and what to do? I found myself jotting down what worked well (getting muddy in puddles) and what didn't (pressing flowers). I wrote notes about what to pack (extra socks) and what I could leave at home (my nice coat). I chatted to friends about the right carriers and the best buggies, while I read up on our local edible greens and the habits of tortoises (one of whom became our pet, Gerald). My husband, Duncan, joined in the challenge, and started contributing ideas and time towards it. Somewhere along the line he also became my writing partner, and made a sizeable contribution to this book.

The quest became just as much our children's as it was ours: they found what worked for them, which outfits, which accessories, which activities and locations. They asked us, repeatedly, to explore certain areas, like our local stream, while remaining completely unmoved by others. They took it upon themselves to build and take down their own shelter, several times. At the end of the day, though, they remained enthusiastic and happy to explore a variety of different activities. On most days, more so than us adults!

A year outside: the challenge

As the book formed in my mind and our visits to the outdoors became more regular, I devised a tool that I thought would help me get out more: A Year Outside Challenge. It was pretty simple really. Starting on 1 January we committed, as a family, to spend at least half an hour a day outside, for a year. Everything counted: from being in the garden, to a walk round the block. It wasn't *what* we did, it was that we did it out of doors.

Most of the time it was easy. But then there were the 'tough' days. Wind and rain was only part of the difficulty. Sometimes, even on a clear day I would struggle to get everything 'together' enough to leave the house. Other days would be a challenge for other reasons, like the day our front door lock broke (shut) and the only way out was through the window (that lasted three days – the kids thought it was hilarious. My poor back was not as impressed.) Or the two consecutive days of flat tyres that threw our plans into a tailspin.

Overall we managed, and as the challenge wore on, I found myself picking up automatic routines that only helped. Having a pre-packed outing bag, for one. And getting the right clothes for most weather. Our attitude changed too – the boys came to expect going out, usually first thing in the morning, no matter what. And I became less likely to find excuses and instead tried to find solutions. Reading all the research into the benefits of being outdoors, no matter what the weather, was definitely an extra incentive, so I share some of the highlights here. I hope it inspires you to get out there too!

The book is written in two parts: the first outlines some of the scientific research on the benefits of being outdoors, the psychological and physical aspects, as well as the way being and playing in nature can be character building. The second is a record of our year outside, by season, and it is full of activities that you can try out with your children. Finally, in the appendix you will find some handy tips on building your own effective outdoor environment in your garden. That's not to say the book must be read in this order, and, as should be the case for a book meant for parents of young children who don't have time to read a book from cover to cover, *Growing Up Wild* has been written so that it can be read in short bursts. You can dip in and out of it, as you wish, either using the index, or looking up activities by season.

What counts as natural or outdoors

Nature does not have to be remote or pristine. It does not have to be perfect or unspoilt and it does not have to be all-encompassing. Several studies have found that even a little nature can be beneficial to our mental state.

For example, patients recovering from surgery who looked out onto green landscapes and trees were found to recover faster than those who could see brick walls.[1] Similarly, students seemed to be more satisfied with their lives when they studied in greener campuses[2] and nurses who took their breaks outdoors, in a natural space, reported being refreshed, relaxed and energised upon returning to work, 'almost as if they were starting the day again'.[3]

For the purposes of this book we have used 'nature' to include all possible varieties of natural environment: beach and lakeside, parks and forests, private and public gardens. Urban nature, very

1 Ulrich, R. (1984). View through a window may influence recovery from surgery. *Science*, *224*(4647), 224–5.
2 McFarland, A. L., Waliczek, T. M., & Zajicek, J. M. (2008). The relationship between student use of campus green spaces and perceptions of quality of life. *HortTechnology*, *18*(2), 232–8.
3 Irvine, K., & Warber, S. L. (2003). Work breaks and well-being: the effect of nature on hospital nurses. *Dissertation abstracts international.*

much present in most UK cities, with a variety of ecosystems co-existing with humans and merging man-made and natural, often seamlessly, is a good start. Local parks, village greens, towpaths and commons can be utilised and provide a varied 'diet' of natural environments.

In praise of the back garden

Even the smallest outdoor space can be of benefit. In fact my personal experience with having two little ones, but in teaching as well, was that often it was the smallest of spaces that were the easiest to navigate, while also offering the same benefits as larger spots.

For some of the activities you don't even need a garden: a paved outdoor space can work just as well (for example, gardening or bird feeding). In one of the schools where I taught, in Greater London, space was at a premium and we simply did most of our gardening in pots, in a rather cramped outdoor paved space. Granted, the children would have benefited more from a lush, spacious garden, but they still enjoyed it and reaped several of the benefits associated with gardening, planting, growing and even cooking with and serving their own herbs and vegetables. Equally, the local, rather modest, green was used for a lot of outdoor activities, and very successfully too.

Similarly, with a toddler and a preschooler at home, our back garden became one of the default outdoor spaces. Led by Duncan's creative flair and handiness, our medium-sized back garden became an engaging and natural play space. In the chapter about effective outdoor spaces for children, he has written about some ideas on how to maximise even the smallest outdoor space. For me, it meant that on the days when getting everyone dressed and ready to go was more than I could handle, all I had to do was open the back door and venture a mere few metres outside of it, sometimes in my pyjamas.

PART ONE:

THE SCIENCE BIT – BENEFITS OF OUTSIDE

CHAPTER 1

Happier outdoors – mental well-being

You are walking your dog when your phone buzzes. You stop, make a note of how happy you feel and then continue on with your day. At the same time your phone – using GPS technology – tracks and records your location. The data is then compiled along with information from another 20,000 participants and is analysed by researchers George MacKerron and Susana Mourato. What they find might not be that surprising, but it confirms something that scientists and laypeople have suspected for ages: we are happier when outdoors, in green spaces, than in urban environments. What's more, we are happiest when we are near the sea, regardless of weather, company or activity.[1] Making the most of modern technology and our love of our personal mobile devices, the scientists looked at over a million responses, using an app to link GPS data and momentary subjective well-being, or to put it simply how happy we feel at each moment in time.

1 MacKerron, G., & Mourato, S. (2013). Happiness is greater in natural environments. *Global environmental change*, *23*(5), 992–1000.

The researchers put forward three possible theories to explain this effect. The first is *biophilia,* the hypothesis that we have evolved to have an instinctive bond with nature, and all living things in it. Indeed, as the authors of the study suggest, there are distinct responses that humans have to natural environments, including stress reduction and attention restoration. These two effects could be central to our elevated mood when we are outside.

Secondly, when compared to urban settings, natural environments are a lot lower in what can be identified as negatives: noise and air pollution, traffic dangers and constant movement. Studies show that chronic exposure to these can affect us both physically and emotionally, raising our stress levels and associated markers, like blood pressure and sleep disturbances.[1] Subconsciously or not, our perceptions of pollution and noise also seem to affect our happiness levels. So, being in quiet, tranquil environments tends to remove these stimuli and help us become calm and feel rebalanced.

Finally, being outdoors can simply be linked to other positive behaviours. We are more likely to exercise, for example, have positive social interactions or take part in fun activities out of doors than inside. All these add up to making the time we spend outside happier!

1 Passchier-Vermeer, W., & Passchier, W. F. (2000). Noise exposure and public health. *Environmental health perspectives, 108*(Suppl 1), 123.

Attention Restoration Theory – nature's prescription

Have you ever noticed just how relaxed you feel after being in a forest, or after a walk in the park? Rachel and Stephen Kaplan, two psychology professors from the University of Michigan, have studied just this feeling of 'restoration' for the last forty years. Their theory is fairly intuitive, but has also been tested widely. It posits that most of everyday life requires our focused attention – from crossing the road to working on our computers, we need to focus solely on one thing, directing our attention to it to the exclusion of a lot of other stimuli.[1] This directed attention, which is of course very beneficial in its own way and vital for our survival and productivity, can cause mental fatigue. Exposure to natural environments can counteract this fatigue; in a way it is a direct remedy for it.

The theory therefore emphasises the restorative effect of effortless attention that can be found in natural environments. The effortless attention in nature is full of what the authors call 'soft fascinations': the rustling leaves, bubbling streams and chirping birds. Time in green and natural spaces, spent in this effortless state, directly counteracts the focused attention that so permeates our everyday

1 Kaplan, R., & Kaplan, S. (1989). *The experience of nature: A psychological perspective*. CUP Archive.

life. Children seem to be particularly affected when too much focused attention is not balanced by enough effortless attention.

Numerous studies have looked at just that: how nature can have a restorative effect on children's attention and have a sustained positive impact on their physical and psychological well-being. A specific link between Attention Deficit Hyperactivity Disorder (ADHD) and green, outdoor spaces has been studied on several occasions and more rigorous trials are now expected.

One US-based study analysed evidence from everyday play settings. The findings suggest that children who suffer from ADHD seem to have milder symptoms when they play in greener play settings, as compared to children who play in urban and built environments.[1] It's not the first time this effect has been seen and researchers from the University of Illinois go so far as to suggest that being in greener spaces can be seen as a 'potential natural treatment for ADHD'.[2]

So, would moving to a greener neighbourhood improve your child's cognitive functioning? One US study tried to look at this: by comparing children's attention test scores pre- and post-move the researchers tried to see if a change of home environment to a greener neighbourhood

1 Faber Taylor, A., & Kuo, F. E. (2011). Could exposure to everyday green spaces help treat ADHD? Evidence from children's play settings. *Applied Psychology: Health and Well-Being*, *3*(3), 281–303.
2 Kuo, F. E., & Faber Taylor, A. (2004). A potential natural treatment for attention-deficit/hyperactivity disorder: evidence from a national study. *American journal of public health*, *94*(9), 1580–6.

was linked to changes in cognitive functioning. The researchers report that: 'Children who experienced the most improvement (increase) in the natural elements or restorative characteristics of their home tended to have the greatest ability to direct their attention and focus several months after moving to the new home.'[1] The findings echo a much older study on college students, which found that natural views from one's dorm window were positively associated with better performance on several tests that measure attention and focus.[2]

Although more research needs to be done in order to untangle the cause and effect of such interventions, scheduling in some green time for our children can be easy, fun and side-effect free. A walk in the park, outdoor play, climbing a tree or gardening for an hour a day can be a worthwhile goal, with surprising benefits for our minds, as well as our bodies.

Dirty, happy kids

Swava, a childminder of over twenty years' experience, who has worked with many kids and families once told me this, and it

1 Wells, N. M. (2000). At home with nature: effects of 'greenness' on children's cognitive functioning. *Environment and behavior*, *32*(6), 775–95.
2 Tennessen, C. M., & Cimprich, B. (1995). Views to nature: Effects on attention. *Journal of environmental psychology*, *15*(1), 77–85.

stuck with me. 'There are two types of children in the world, Alexia,' she said. 'Those who are happy,' she paused for effect, 'and those who are clean.' It resonated with me then – and made me feel a little better about the state of my little ones, who spend a very tiny amount of their day clean, namely the ten minutes after they come out of the bath – but as I started looking at some research it also seems to be almost literally true!

Research coming out of the University of Bristol and University College London suggests that there is a certain friendly bacterium found in soil, *Mycobacterium vaccae*, that could affect the brain in a similar way to antidepressants.[1] The researchers got interested in this bacterium when they found out that cancer patients treated with it reported an improvement in their quality of life. They subsequently studied mice treated with the bacterium, to find that a special set of neurons were activated to release more serotonin.

Serotonin, a neurotransmitter, is found in the gut, central nervous system and blood platelets of humans and it is thought to contribute to feelings of happiness. Drugs that alter serotonin levels are used to treat conditions such as depression and anxiety. Playing on and digging in soil may expose children (and adults) to

1 Lowry, C. A., Hollis, J. H., de Vries, A., Pan, B., Brunet, L. R., Hunt, J. R., . . . & Lightman, S. L. (2007). Identification of an immune-responsive mesolimbocortical serotonergic system: potential role in regulation of emotional behavior. *Neuroscience*, *146*(2), 756–72.

this and other friendly bacteria that could enhance well-being, as well as boost our children's immune system (p. 24). The lead researcher and author of the paper says: '[These studies] leave us wondering if we shouldn't all be spending more time playing in the dirt.'[1] And while you or I might not be able to quit our job and spend our days in the garden, young children should have ready access to natural environments, to soil and dirt and, why not, mud!

You are my sunshine

How would you feel about going to a café, where for a small amount of money you could be exposed to 'intense natural light' while you drink your beverage? Light cafés, or light therapy cafés do just that. Sitting in front of a light box for thirty minutes to an hour a day can help alleviate seasonal affective disorder (SAD) – a mood disorder caused by the reduced amount of natural light in winter. Even the Royal College of Psychiatrists agree that there is some evidence to support the use of light boxes.[2]

1 http://www.bristol.ac.uk/news/2007/5384.html accessed 24 April 2016
2 http://www.rcpsych.ac.uk/healthadvice/problemsdisorders/seasonalaffectivedisorder.aspx accessed 6 July 2016

But why is that? Why do we get SAD (and sad) in winter and can we do anything other than visit light cafés? It seems that up until a couple of generations ago most people spent a substantial part of their day outside, working in fields, in animal husbandry or, even before that, foraging and hunting. With that in mind, we have evolved to be outdoors and there is now evidence to suggest that we are a lot happier when we spend our time exposed to natural light.

The benefits of light exposure to our mood have been studied a lot, and alterations on levels of neurotransmitters (chemicals in our brains), seem to be central to seasonal mood variations, including SAD. Indeed, researchers have found that the rate of production of serotonin, the neurotransmitter that is linked with mood, rises rapidly with increased luminosity,[1] meaning that more light could improve our mood. The same piece of research found that serotonin levels were lowest in winter, when light levels naturally drop, on top of which, most of us prefer to be inside with a cup of coffee, rather than out facing the elements.

Here's an interesting thought though: unless you live in the Arctic Circle, even on the most cloudy of days and even in the middle of winter, the light outside during daytime is normally above 1,000 lux, a level that cannot be achieved indoors. And yet most of us

1 Lambert, G. W., Reid, C., Kaye, D. M., Jennings, G. L., & Esler, M. D. (2002). Effect of sunlight and season on serotonin turnover in the brain. *The Lancet, 360*(9348), 1840–2.

spend increasingly more and more time indoors, deprived of natural, bright light.

Time spent outside in even cloudy weather can have similar effects to time spent outside on brighter days. Adding exercise to the mix can multiply the positive effect, as physical exertion is also linked to raised serotonin levels.[1] Indeed in a large study of other studies (a systematic review) that compared the benefits of physical activity in indoor vs outdoor natural environments, it was found that both mental and physical well-being were enhanced further when exercise took place in natural surroundings.[2] More specifically the report found some positive effects of outdoor exercise on self-reported mental well-being immediately following exercise in nature, which do not occur when the exercise took place indoors.

Unsurprisingly, perhaps, several studies show that we all tend to be more active when we are outside. Children are no exception: a study using accelerometers, which measure movement, on children aged between six and eleven found that they were active 41 per cent of the time that they spent

1 Young, S. N. (2007). How to increase serotonin in the human brain without drugs. *Journal of psychiatry & neuroscience: JPN*, *32*(6), 394.
2 Thompson Coon, J., Boddy, K., Stein, K., Whear, R., Barton, J., & Depledge, M. H. (2011). Does participating in physical activity in outdoor natural environments have a greater effect on physical and mental wellbeing than physical activity indoors? A systematic review. *Environmental science & technology*, *45*(5), 1761–72.

out of doors, compared to 18 per cent of the time when they were indoors.[1] Time spent outdoors also has a positive effect on overall fitness outcomes.[2] Which moves us onto the physical benefits of being outside.

1 Kneeshaw-Price, S., Saelens, B.E., Sallis, J.F., Glanz, K., Frank, L., . . . & Cain, K. (2013) Children's objective physical activity by location: why the neighborhood matters. *Pediatric exercise science*; 25 (3): 468–86.
2 Gray, C., Gibbons, R., Larouche, R., et al. What is the relationship between outdoor time and physical activity, sedentary behaviour, and physical fitness in children? A systematic review (2015). *International Journal of Environmental Research and Public Health*.

CHAPTER 2

The physical benefits

More than just affecting our mental health, being close to nature also has very real benefits for our physical selves. We have been, over the last hundred years, effectively moving away from outdoor pursuits in our daily lives, from farming and hunting, into a more indoor existence. At the same time, some of us have started to actively choose the outdoors as a place to spend our leisure time. A variety of pastimes have captured our imagination, from hiking and camping, to trail running and bird watching – many imitating our lives as hunter-gatherers or nomadic people – and it seems that many of these activities have unexpected benefits, on several levels.

Shinrin-yoku or forest bathing

None of the activities I have looked at, however, quite capture the gentle balance between mental, spiritual and physical benefits of choosing to spend time in nature, as completely as the Japanese practice of 'Shinrin-yoku', roughly translated as forest bathing. Simply put, Shinrin-yoku involves taking a short, relaxed walk in a natural space with the senses very much open to take in the atmosphere around you. It is an experience that is meant to encompass mind and body, to soothe and revitalise. Taking in the forest atmosphere should ideally involve most senses, with smell and hearing being at the forefront.

Forest bathing has been endorsed and actively proposed by the Ministry of Health of Japan since 1982 as a health habit that should be incorporated into a good lifestyle. In the period since then a number of studies have tried to analyse the host of positive effects relating to this gentle nature walk, including a research paper[1] published by the Japanese Department of Hygiene and Public Health. This outlined both psychological and physiological changes that can lead to an overall healthier life and increased well-being, including changes in the immune system and improvement of mood.

Other studies suggest that even the smallest details, like the essential oils found in the wood of many trees, especially pines and other conifers, have a positive influence on our health. Phytoncides, these essential oils, seem to have a positive effect on

1 Li, Q., Morimoto, K., Kobayashi, M., Inagaki, H., Katsumata, M., Hirata, Y., . . . & Kawada, T. (2008). Visiting a forest, but not a city, increases human natural killer activity and expression of anti-cancer proteins. *International journal of immunopathology and pharmacology*, *21*(1), 117–27.

our immune system, boosting natural killer cell production.[1] Some trails in Japan are certified as having high levels of phytoncides, and therefore particularly suited to the practice of forest bathing.

More research, which compared the practice of walking and simply observing in a forest versus urban environments showed that 'forest environments promote lower concentrations of cortisol, lower pulse rate, lower blood pressure, greater parasympathetic nerve activity, and lower sympathetic nerve activity than do city environments.'[2]

Forest bathing has been gaining ground steadily in western countries, especially the US, where people increasingly feel the need to unplug and recharge in nature. It has even been described by some as the 'latest fitness trend' and compared to other eastern practices that have become mainstream, such as yoga and meditation.[3] The evidence that supports this as a beneficial way to spend your leisure time is certainly coming in thick and fast: forest bathing is good for our mental and physical health too!

1 Li, Q., Nakadai, A., Matsushima, H., Miyazaki, Y., Krensky, A. M., Kawada, T. & Morimoto, K. (2006). Phytoncides (wood essential oils) induce human natural killer cell activity. *Immunopharmacology and immunotoxicology*, *28*(2), 319–33.
2 Park, B. J., Tsunetsugu, Y., Kasetani, T., Kagawa, T., & Miyazaki, Y. (2010). The physiological effects of Shinrin-yoku (taking in the forest atmosphere or forest bathing): evidence from field experiments in 24 forests across Japan. *Environmental health and preventive medicine*, *15*(1), 18–26.
3 https://www.washingtonpost.com/news/to-your-health/wp/2016/05/17/forest-bathing-is-latest-fitness-trend-to-hit-u-s-where-yoga-was-30-years-ago/ accessed 10 August 2016

Outdoors and eyesight

After several months of digging deep into the scientific literature trying to find all of the benefits that time outdoors might offer our kids, I was amazed to find that my mother might have been right all along when she said I should not spend all that time in front of the TV for fear my eyes would be affected! So when I read that there might be a link between outdoor play and incidences of near-sightedness, I had to know more.

The first study I came across was a review of many other studies in this field, with a combined total of over 10,000 participants. It was presented at the 115th Annual Meeting of the American Academy of Ophthalmologists and concludes that children who spend more time outside tend to have better eyesight. More specifically, near-sighted children spend on average 3.7 fewer hours per week engaged in outdoor activities than children with perfect vision or far-sightedness. On top of that, for every hour that children spend outdoors per week, their risk of developing myopia (near-sightedness) drops by about 2 per cent.[1]

In an article in the acclaimed scientific journal *Nature* titled 'The myopia boom' I was surprised to find out that up to 90 per cent of

1 http://www.livescience.com/16693-outdoor-time-lowers-nearsightedness-risk.html accessed 6 July 2016

East Asian youth are affected by short-sightedness.[1] It's not just East Asia that is affected, though, with about half of young adults in Europe and the US also having the condition. To compare, sixty years ago the prevalence was a lot lower at 10–20 per cent (although this might be partly influenced by more effective diagnosis nowadays). Even so, when looking at potential factors for this, less time outdoors seems like a credible one.

Low level lighting indoors, versus natural light, has been proposed as a potential mechanism, although scientists have been cautious about oversimplifying the reasons behind the condition. Yet, clearly, there is a generational difference, and when looking for the cause, time spent indoors seems to be at least part of it.

This is not something entirely new; indeed researchers have documented the link between 'being bookish' and prevalence of the condition since the 1990s.[2] Yet, when looking at the variability of time spent reading, or other close work, the association did not seem to hold. Another factor did, though, and it was time spent outdoors!

The epidemiological data was fairly clear: children who spent more time outdoors had better eyesight. It wasn't physical activity

1 Dolgin, E. (2015). The myopia boom. *Nature*, *519*(7543), 276–8.
2 Zylbermann, R., Landau, D., & Berson, D. (1993). The influence of study habits on myopia in Jewish teenagers. *Journal of pediatric ophthalmology and strabismus*, *30*(5), 319–22.

that was behind it, as the effect was lost when children took part in indoor sport. The magic ingredient seemed to be . . . light. Further experimental evidence, from monkeys, shrews and chicks seemed to support the hypothesis – and a plausible mechanism was suggested: natural light stimulated dopamine release in the retina.[1] Lack of sufficient natural light, at least during the day, disrupted the natural cycle of growth in the eye.

Several interventions aimed at improving eyesight with outdoor time are being tested, but the bottom line is that getting our children out and about is beneficial in more ways than we have so far imagined. And sunlight seems to be at the centre of a lot of these benefits. Although we have, for years, been alerted to the dangers of extensive sun exposure, being outdoors and exposed to sunlight in a sensible way is now being linked with optimal health in several ways. One of those is the production of vitamin D.

Precious vitamin D

It turns out that vitamin D is not one single substance, but many. Moreover, I was surprised to learn that vitamin D is not a vitamin,

1 Ashby, R. S., & Schaeffel, F. (2010). The effect of bright light on lens compensation in chicks. *Investigative ophthalmology & visual science*, *51*(10), 5247–53.

as such, as it breaks several 'vitamin rules'.[1] That's because it is produced in the human body, and more specifically in the skin, from a compound called 7-dehydrocholesterol. The key to this conversion process is, you guessed it, sunlight. Ultraviolet B (UVB) light converts 7-dehydrocholesterol into D3, which is what our body then uses to keep us healthy in all sorts of ways.

And it seems that vitamin D is important in more ways than we might have initially thought: it doesn't only keep our bones healthy (where it has a crucial role in calcium absorption). New research is uncovering far-reaching effects that vitamin D has for our body, from links to muscle strength and heart health all the way to fighting the common cold, cancer and type 1 diabetes.[2] A lot of these links are based on epidemiological data, mostly by looking at different rates of occurrence of these conditions in countries close to the Equator, where vitamin D deficiencies are very rare due to regular sun exposure, versus northern countries. However, it should be noted that there are several studies which are now starting to look at plausible mechanisms of the involvement of vitamin D in many of the aforementioned conditions. As the epidemiological data that we have is only correlational, meaning that they don't in themselves explain a cause and effect or mechanism of action, these studies should

1 http://www.health.harvard.edu/mens-health/vitamin-d-and-your-health accessed 9 August 2016
2 https://www.hsph.harvard.edu/nutritionsource/vitamin-d/#new-vitamin-d-research accessed 9 August 2016

help us clarify the role vitamin D might play in keeping us healthy and happy.

For our part, it is a good idea to make sure that we, and our children, get enough hours of sunlight to boost our vitamin D levels naturally, although supplements can, of course, be prescribed by your GP if they feel you need them.

One final word should be written about the links between sunscreen use and vitamin D deficiencies. Theoretically, sunscreen blocks UVB rays that lead to burning and sun damage but also aid in the formation of vitamin D. In practical terms, however, several studies, including a methodologically very sound randomised controlled trial, have shown that sunscreen use is not linked to lower levels of vitamin D.[1 2] A British study, in fact, concludes that: 'Although sunscreens can significantly reduce the production of vitamin D under very strictly controlled conditions, their normal usage does not generally result in vitamin D insufficiency.'[3] That's probably because most of us are not too

1 Marks, R., Foley, P. A., Jolley, D., Knight, K. R., Harrison, J., & Thompson, S. C. (1995). The effect of regular sunscreen use on vitamin D levels in an Australian population: results of a randomized controlled trial. *Archives of dermatology, 131*(4), 415–21.
2 Bhan, A., Rao, A. D., & Rao, D. S. (2010). Osteomalacia as a result of vitamin D deficiency. *Endocrinology and metabolism clinics of North America, 39*(2), 321–31.
3 Norval, M., & Wulf, H. C. (2009). Does chronic sunscreen use reduce vitamin D production to insufficient levels? *British journal of dermatology,161*(4), 732–6.

strict with our sunscreen application, both in terms of time intervals and skin coverage. As sun damage and skin cancer are a concern for many who are regularly exposed to the sun, it is a relief to hear that we can stay safe, by using sunscreen, without forgoing our vitamin D production, which is certainly one of the benefits of being outside.

The 'hygiene hypothesis'

I was naturally drawn to the hygiene hypothesis, perhaps because my house cleaning leaves a lot to be desired. Plus, with three dogs sharing our home and garden, there is never a shortage of dog hair and dander on our floor and furnishings, no matter how often the vacuum cleaner makes an appearance.

The idea that 'dirt is good', or rather that some exposure to microbes, dust and other potential allergens, especially in early childhood, is beneficial in that it helps build a healthy immune system was first formulated by David Strachan in 1990, and linked (positively) to family size, as well as (negatively) to improved home cleanliness and hygiene.[1]

1 Strachan, D. P. (2000). Family size, infection and atopy: the first decade of the 'hygiene hypothesis'. *Thorax*, *55*(Suppl 1), S2.

There have been several studies trying to unweave the complex interaction between environment, hygiene, pet ownership, early childhood infection and both allergic and chronic inflammatory disorders, with no clear conclusion. Some data points to a link between exposure to allergens, including mouse dander and cockroach droppings (!) in infanthood with a diminished likelihood of developing asthma later on.[1]

There seems to be a host of epidemiological data too, looking at different areas of the world and incidences of various allergies, as well as longitudinal data – that's to say data from looking at people over a long period of time – measuring changes in rates of allergies and autoimmune disease occurrence. A study from Ghana, for example, collecting data on asthma and allergies ten years apart reports that incidence of both increased over the ten-year period, especially in urban rich environments.[2]

Closer to home (for me) I was particularly pleased to see the results of a study looking at lifetime pet ownership and prevalence of allergies. Most studies to date had only looked at childhood outcomes, but this one went a little further: it took data from birth

1 Lynch, S. V., Wood, R. A., Boushey, H., Bacharier, L. B., Bloomberg, G. R., Kattan, M., . . . & Johnson, C. C. (2014). Effects of early-life exposure to allergens and bacteria on recurrent wheeze and atopy in urban children. *Journal of Allergy and Clinical Immunology, 134*(3), 593–601.
2 Addo-Yobo, E. O., Woodcock, A., Allotey, A., Baffoe-Bonnie, B., Strachan, D., & Custovic, A. (2007). Exercise-induced bronchospasm and atopy in Ghana: two surveys ten years apart. *PLoS Med,4*(2), e70.

to eighteen to see whether there was any significant difference in asthma and allergy prevalence to children being exposed to cats and dogs.[1] The results were interesting, in that growing up with a dog or cat seemed to have little or no effect *unless* it was in the first year of life. The scientists in the study propose that there might be a 'critical period during childhood when indoor exposure to dogs or cats influences sensitization to these animals'.[2] Interestingly, another study found that living with dogs who spend at least some time outdoors has a bigger effect in protecting children from childhood upper respiratory illness and ear infections than sharing a home with an indoor-only pet.[3]

Another recent study on Amish and Hutterite children has shown the potential protective effect of growing up on certain types of farms when it comes to asthma.[4] The two communities that the scientists looked at had significant differences in the way that they

1 Wegienka, G., Johnson, C. C., Havstad, S., Ownby, D. R., Nicholas, C., & Zoratti, E. M. (2011). Lifetime dog and cat exposure and dog – and cat – specific sensitization at age 18 years. *Clinical & experimental allergy*, *41*(7), 979–86.
2 Wegienka, G., Johnson, C. C., Havstad, S., Ownby, D. R., Nicholas, C., & Zoratti, E. M. (2011). Lifetime dog and cat exposure and dog – and cat – specific sensitization at age 18 years. *Clinical & experimental allergy*, *41*(7), 979.
3 Bergroth, E., Remes, S., Pekkanen, J., Kauppila, T., Büchele, G., & Keski-Nisula, L. (2012). Respiratory tract illnesses during the first year of life: effect of dog and cat contacts. *Pediatrics*, 211–20.
4 Stein, M. M., Hrusch, C. L., Gozdz, J., Igartua, C., Pivniouk, V., Murray, S. E., . . . & Neilson, J. W. (2016). Innate Immunity and Asthma Risk in Amish and Hutterite Farm Children. *New England journal of medicine*, *375*(5), 411–21.

farmed. The Amish, living in single-family farms, where no technology was used, had children who have daily contact with farm animals. The Hutterites, on the other hand, have larger industrialised farms, where children's contact with the livestock was much lower. By comparing asthma prevalence in the two diverse communities, scientists were trying to unravel the relationship of contact with farm animals and the chance of developing asthma. The results were very striking – with Amish children having a far lower prevalence of asthma and differing in their immune response to the Hutterite children. Moreover, when dust from Amish houses, loaded with bacterial debris, was inhaled by mice, their immune response changed! The same wasn't true of Hutterite dust, leading researchers to think that there is something about certain types of microbes and at certain concentrations, that strengthens the immune system and protects against extreme immune reactions, and protects from immune overreactions, i.e. allergies.

Although the evidence for dirty houses protecting against allergies is not conclusive – much to my disappointment – I was happy to see at least that a reasonable amount of dust and animal dander is not damaging to children. Moreover, if you don't have a pet, similar benefits can probably be gained by being outdoors in natural environments.

Sleep tight at night

I am yet to meet a parent who would not wish for better quality, more restorative sleep for themselves and their little ones. Quite often, it seems, one of the biggest challenges of parenting young children revolves around the daily habit of naps and bedtimes. As a mum of two young kids, I spent rather a long time trying to work out the elusive answer to better night-time sleeps. I have endlessly fiddled with naptimes, bringing them back and forward and noting their effect. I have gone from blackout blinds and no noise, to white noise and a strict bath–bedtime routine, as well as various combinations of pre-sleep meals and snacks. But in the end it seems that the most effective change for my family is supported by plenty of science: outdoor time in the morning helps everyone sleep better!

There are two reported mechanisms through which outdoor time promotes sound sleep: one is increased physical activity, which is something all mums know – the more your little ones run around in the day the more likely they are to have a good night's sleep. The other is related to natural light exposure: our diurnal clocks are set by our exposure to light, making us more likely to want to nod off when it's dark and wake up when it's light. This effect can be seen as early as a few weeks of age. A particular study in infants aged six to twelve weeks found that babies who were exposed to more afternoon light slept significantly better at night.[1]

And of course, more and better sleep, the holy grail of parenthood, is linked to all sorts of positive outcomes, from optimum growth, to increased school performance, more stable moods, better mental health and finally better weight regulation.[2] On top of that, while the kids sleep you can get your own zzzs in, read a book in silence, or, if you really have to, catch up on housework. What's not to like?

1 Harrison, Y. (2004). The relationship between daytime exposure to light and night-time sleep in 6–12-week-old infants. *Journal of sleep research*, *13*(4), 345–52.

2 http://www.nwf.org/News-and-Magazines/Media-Center/News-by-Topic/Get-Outside/2011/09-06-11-Sleep-Report.aspx accessed 13 July 2016

CHAPTER 3

Character building

Risky outdoor play and social/ emotional competencies

Aside from the physical and psychological benefits, outdoor play has even more to offer. Risky play, by definition, provides opportunities for challenge, testing limits, exploring boundaries and learning about injury risk.[1] And although the benefits of risky play are many, this sentence from a systematic review (a study of studies) on risky play brings me back to my senses: 'risky outdoor play has been associated with promoting children's health and development, but also with injury and death'.[2] This gets me thinking, and reading more.

1 Sandseter, E. B. H. (2007). Risky play among four- and five-year-old children in preschool. *Vision into practice: Making quality a reality in the lives of young children*, 248–56.
2 Brussoni, M., Gibbons, R., Gray, C., Ishikawa, T., Sandseter, E. B. H., Bienenstock, A., . . . & Pickett, W. (2015). What is the relationship between risky outdoor play and health in children? A systematic review. *International journal of environmental research and public health, 12*(6), 6423–54.

The study, overall, has a positive message as regards risky outdoor play: it leads to higher levels of physical activity and health, while it also seems to have an effect on social interactions, creativity and resilience. Yet, there is no doubt that there are dangers too. I want to know how to strike a balance, so I get reading and chatting to the experts.

In a paper titled 'The risk that there is no risk' researchers describe how overzealous risk reduction can handicap our kids, by taking away any element of excitement or challenge and greatly limiting what children can do.[1] By adding materials of no fixed purpose (like car tyres or boxes) to a playground, the researchers found that children not only engaged with them more, but also became significantly more active. Other studies have produced similar results that leave us with the same conclusion: risky play has an overall positive impact on a host of parameters in young kids.

And what about injury? Well, it's a risk. However, some studies have found that children are more likely to be injured in adult-directed activities (such as organised sport) rather than in free, risky play, when they actively manage the risks themselves. I chat with Mike, a PE teacher and outdoor enthusiast, who seems to support the above theory. In his experience too, children are more

1 Bundy, A. C., Luckett, T., Tranter, P. J., Naughton, G. A., Wyver, S. R., Ragen, J., & Spies, G. (2009). The risk is that there is 'no risk': a simple, innovative intervention to increase children's activity levels. *International journal of early years education*, *17*(1), 33–45.

likely to be injured playing sport, than hiking, climbing or building shelters on the mountain. In fact, he shares with me that in his eighteen years of coaching sport as well as leading expeditions in the wild, he has made less than ten trips to A&E, with only one being from an outdoor expedition related incident – the rest were all fractures or concussions sustained on the football or rugby pitch. 'Children are more sensible in the wild,' he tells me, 'and more likely to avoid unnecessary risks.'

There are, however, ways to minimise *some* risks – those that could result in serious injury – while letting kids manage other, smaller and more manageable risks. Guidelines have been developed that can help adults identify and remove more serious risks, while other hazards are viewed as acceptable – both because of their developmental benefits, but also because they can be perceived by children themselves who can then adjust their own behaviour.[1] For our part, being around our children, having a well-stocked first aid kit and a charged mobile phone is always a good idea.

There is also a lot to be said about the development of social and emotional competencies in young kids during outdoor play. A whole host of emotions arise when children engage in risky outdoor play. The thrill and exhilaration that children get is a

1 Play England http://dera.ioe.ac.uk/8625/1/00942-2008DOM-EN.pdf accessed 26 July 2016

combination of freedom and fear. And yet, as parents, we often don't want our children to experience fear.

Fear is often seen as a negative emotion. We forget that it has played a significant role throughout our evolution and children need to learn how to deal with the experience of fear – to control it, and to listen to it. Risky play does just that: it gives our kids a sense of their own boundaries. Only by testing those boundaries, by going close enough to the edge to see the drop, can they start making decisions for themselves.

There is a theory in psychology that links play with the ability to learn self-regulation: that is, the ability to regulate emotions such as fear and anger.[1] When our children engage in risky play, they are free to experience appropriate levels of these feelings. They thus learn to manage them successfully, and on their own. When this play is also social they can learn to manage such emotions in their interactions with others too. By learning to regulate these emotions they are immediately rewarded by being able to continue to play: losing one's cool would naturally and automatically lead to one being temporarily excluded from play.

The advantages of such social development is what we call 'character building'. Self-regulation is, after all, one of the most

1 LaFreniere, P. (2011). Evolutionary functions of social play: Life histories, sex differences, and emotion regulation. *American journal of play, 3*, 464–88.

important skills our children can possess. Learning to deal with our frustrations, from the little things that bug us, to the big things that make us angry and get our blood boiling, is a skill that stays with us for ever. Moreover, it is linked with a host of positive outcomes, including academic success and successful relationships with others.[1 2]

By letting our children engage with nature, engage with its inherent risks in a sensible manner, we offer them the opportunity to develop unique skills. Resilience is one of those, too. By letting them fail, and natural play offers plenty of opportunities for failure, we help them develop a resilient streak – the idea of 'if at first you don't succeed, try and try again' can readily be developed when children engage in natural play.

The outdoors also takes us out of our comfort zone – quite literally! When out in nature we say goodbye to our creature comforts. Whether we are camping or simply out for a long hike we do not have immediate access to all the things that we usually take for granted, including running water, a clean lavatory, any food we like, etc. That alone can be a lesson for kids. For me, personally, it is one of the reasons that, while I go out prepared

1 Dent, A. L. (2013). *The relation between self-regulation and academic achievement: A meta-analysis exploring variation in the way constructs are labeled, defined, and measured* (Doctoral dissertation, Duke University).
2 Fitzsimons, G. M., & Finkel, E. J. (2011). The effects of self-regulation on social relationships. *Handbook of self-regulation: Research, theory, and applications*, 407–21.

with a few drinks and some snacks, I try not to be a 'walking shop'. Temporary limited access to all their favourite things is a good thing once in a while, and it's there to teach us, and our children, to be more grateful for the things that we do have: another reason why connecting with nature and getting outside can be character building.

Finally, outdoor activities can positively impact self-esteem. There is a rare feeling of accomplishment to completing a tough climb, or getting to the top of a tree, to building a shelter or a fire. Such experiences abound in nature and have an impact on the way children look at themselves as competent, able persons.

The beauty of unstructured time – and the challenge of boredom

As a teacher I had seen it again and again: children with schedules so packed they hardly had any time to free play. I was often asked what activities were best, and how to fit violin, tennis and swimming lessons into a week. As a parent I can see it again – even from a very young age, we look to enrich our children's days with all these extra experiences. Babies as young as a few months have classes: for creativity, for swimming and singing and dancing. I appreciate the need for parents to have these, and I am a firm believer in routine, but not at the expense of unstructured, free time.

I guess, as with most things, balance is the key. Organised activities, especially when they offer socialisation, the learning of skills and participation in sport, can definitely have a place and a time in our kids' schedules. However, there is beauty in unstructured time, and even in that dreaded word: boredom.

Boredom can actually have several positive side-effects. Defined by Professor Eastwood, who has been studying boredom for the last ten years, as 'the aversive experience of wanting, but being unable, to engage in satisfying activity'.[1] It seems to be a very common feeling, even amongst the busiest of us. But, when unstructured time multiplies, for example in the summer holidays or after-school, boredom rears its, not necessarily ugly, head. Far from being a negative, boredom can in fact lead us to our true desires. Learning to explore this rather uncomfortable feeling can bring us closer to what we really want to do. With kids too, being given the gift of free time (with limited access to default activities, like TV or computer games), although at first frustrating, can actually lead to the discovery of more fulfilling and truly engaging activities.

1 Eastwood, J. D., Frischen, A., Fenske, M. J. & Smilek, D. (2012). The unengaged mind. *Perspectives on psychological science*, 7(5), 482–95.

A study led by another 'boredom expert', Dr Sandi Mann found that participants who had to carry out a boring activity, like copying out phone numbers from a telephone directory, were a lot more creative when they were presented with a creative task, compared to their non-bored counterparts.[1]

Susanne, mum of two, talks to me about how her seven year old, with a little guidance from her, managed to spend most of a hot Saturday designing, building, decorating and playing with a den in his bedroom. They were both delighted as they talked to me about this new experience of unstructured time.

And here's the first paradox. Parental guidance is not always a dirty word. Yes, we talk of free play and yes, we want our children to be creative. But sometimes, often in fact, we need to show them the way. It might come in the shape of creating opportunities, or providing the right environment – for my little ones a reminder that the sand pit is just outside can work wonders. For Andrew, Susanne's seven-year-old son, his mum's suggestion was not enough – she had to give him some of the materials he could use and start him off. But those twenty minutes of meaningful engagement really set him off and he played happily for hours – creating, using his imagination and truly enjoying his time.

1 Mann, S. & Cadman, R. (2014). Does being bored make us more creative? *Creativity research journal*, 26(2), 165–73.

I also get the feeling that sometimes 'boredom' can be a conscious or subconscious cry for parental attention. And in these cases too, a little can go a long way. By connecting to our kids, by guiding them in their activity and then letting them explore it on their own, we can give them the gift of free, creative play.

A different perspective to this is also important and needs to be balanced with our desire to distract our children. Psychoanalyst Adam Philips writes about this process of boredom and finding a way out of it as a skill that a child must learn, a developmental step.[1] I like that too – the sense that we do not have to, as parents, endlessly entertain or provide entertainment for our kids.

A lot of the activities in this book are a gateway to letting our kids manage their own time and engagement. We provide the impetus, the inspiration and sometimes the materials and let them take charge. There's no direct conflict here: parental guidance is merely a nudge that children often need in order to learn to structure their free time themselves.

For my family, unstructured time is guarded fiercely. I know that there are things to do, places to be, jobs and chores and activities. And so often we end up with this second paradox. The paradox of

1 Philips, A. (1993). *On kissing, tickling and being bored.* Cambridge, MA: Harvard University Press.

actually scheduling in unstructured time. For us, it seems to be the only way to carve it out and guard it – by actually setting it aside.

Environmental education, respect and cultivating connection

Away from scientific studies, but closer to my experience as a professional in education, and also as a keen outdoor enthusiast, is the close link between feeling connected with nature and respecting it. At a time when environmental issues are going to be at the very centre of our children's lives – and most likely their biggest challenges are going to lie just there, in preserving a rapidly declining natural environment – education and the careful cultivation of a relationship with nature is probably part of the answer.

As part of the ecosystem, but in many ways apart from it too, the closer we feel to our natural environment, the more we feel we are an integral part of it. If, in turn, the natural environment is an important part of our lives, the more likely we are to make sacrifices in our way of life in order to protect it. In fact, herein lies another positive: a lifestyle that has nature at its core is more likely to be sustainable in itself. When we look to nature for our leisure, for our spiritual growth and exercise, we are less likely to need a lot of the paraphernalia of the consumerist lifestyle that is part of the problem.

Growing and sustaining an attachment to nature can, and should, be fun. It can start early, in babyhood, and grow with our children, being cemented by every activity that brings us in touch with it, that connects us further. On top of that, by showing our children that we value nature, and by modelling the respect that we want them to have, we are building a more sustainable future. The relationship grows through getting to know diverse environments, far and near, by experiencing the flora and the fauna, by respecting what's there, by being a keen observer and by leaving no trace.

Action follows and, while most of the activities in this book have connection as an aim, some are actually early forerunners of taking action to find solutions and improving our environment. Planting their own vegetables and making bird feeders (p. 92) are child friendly ways to approach sustainability. More actively engaging activities, like organising a beach clean-up can follow.

A small note

Science can be very powerful in helping us find what works and what doesn't. However, when using scientific evidence we have to be cautious. All the sources are valid, and the evidence I use is mostly from peer reviewed journals, with references available for all who want to know more. However, the studies I have included are cherry-picked, and not exhaustive. This is not a systematic review of everything that's out there. Although the majority of studies have been done on adult participants rather than children, the overall evidence, empirical and anecdotal, seems to point towards a positive relationship between nature and well-being.

I am excited to see there are some systematic reviews, that is studies that will look at all the evidence to date, coming out of Exeter University's Medical School. I look forward to their findings.

PART TWO:

THE ACTIVITIES

WINTER

1 *Hiking with kids*

A Year Outside Challenge – day 1

1 January

Weather: Icy, but dry

I'm lying in bed, a soft buzzing in my ears. I feel dreadful: my throat is sore, my back is stiff and my eyes feel like I have been through a sandstorm. I have all the tell-tale signs of a hangover. And yet, a hangover this is not – I was in bed by eleven, missing the New Year's festivities in favour of a little extra sleep. I am sure I'm not the only sleep-deprived parent who chose sleep over champagne for New Year's Eve.

Oliver coos and laughs next to me, his laugh catching in his throat, like only babies' laughs do and coming out all gurgly, bubbling up to the surface, like fresh water from a mountain stream. I lift him out of his cot and place him between me and the seemingly lifeless body next to me. A groan comes from that side of the bed. A genuine, honest-to-god, I-need-more-sleep groan.

It is the first day of the year and as tradition has it we are heading on a hike. We have had little sleep, Oliver is still far from sleeping through the night (twelve hours, what?) and my husband, Duncan, and I are both feeling the effects of more than a year of sleepless nights. Oliver not so much. His brother, Joe, has also woken up full of energy and bursting with life, just as a two and half year old should. The mountain it is then. Never mind the below freezing temperatures and icy roads: we cannot contain these two within the walls of our house. The outdoors offers a release for their energy that cannot be rivalled.

I get up to make some coffee, and look out at the snowy peaks gleaming in the morning sunshine. A.B.

Hiking, hillwalking, countryside rambling. A wonderful way to get in touch with nature, to wind down, walking in the woods is a special privilege – whether it is a great wood or a coppice in a small park. We go to these places for a short visit away from our usual lives. In all ways, it is meant to be different to what we usually see. Whether we are out roughing it for a weekend or on an afternoon's stroll, we want it to be different, untouched and to enjoy the pretence at least of being in the wild.

Duncan and I both enjoyed hiking, but when children were added to the mix, we found that we were a little worried about how to hike with the kids, in ways that were both safe, but also enjoyable. After all, what is the point of a forced hike when no one is enjoying themselves? Or a meltdown when you are two hours from the nearest road?

And yet, hiking trips, when done right, can create some of the fondest memories you can have as a family. Hiking can be a tool for bonding and unwinding together, enjoying nature and simply being present with your family. The benefits of walking, as exercise, are numerous: walking is an ideal low intensity exercise that will strengthen your heart, lower your blood pressure and increase your bone density. It is simple to get started and you don't need any special equipment – though when hiking with kids there are a few items that can definitely make your life easier.

There are wider benefits to hiking too. Researchers from Stanford University found that walking in nature for ninety minutes had an effect on thinking patterns.[1] In particular, they found that self-reported rumination, a type of thinking associated with heightened risk of depression and other mental illness, was markedly decreased when walking in nature. Walking in an urban setting, on

1 Bratman, G. N., Hamilton, J. P., Hahn, K. S., Daily, G. C., & Gross, J. J. (2015). Nature experience reduces rumination and subgenual prefrontal cortex activation. *Proceedings of the National Academy of Sciences, 112*(28), 8567–72.

the other hand, had no such effect. Moreover, they performed brain scans to look at neural activity in a specific area of the brain, the subgenual prefrontal cortex – an area associated with self-focused behavioural withdrawal linked to rumination in both depressed and healthy individuals. The researchers conclude that walking in nature, and providing adequate natural environments within urban contexts, may be vital for our mental health.

Find out what motivates *your* kids – my little ones don't care about views or reaching somewhere, it seems they are more interested in the process, and finding things along the way: stop to look at the fox hole, or a strangely shaped rock, count how many beetles we see along the way, or go from berry bush to berry bush. This change of perspective is at first difficult, but makes us see the hike with fresh eyes. Hiking in the company of slightly older children keeps the little ones moving along at a faster pace, keen to keep up with the 'big kids'.

SNACKS AND DRINKS

Allowing children to have their own backpacks with snacks and a bottle of water can give them a little sense of autonomy and choice, which can go a long way. However, be prepared that you might, at some point, have to carry the backpack, or in fact, the backpack *and* the child.

Regular stops for a bite or a sip are a must and can sometimes be a motivating factor to keep everyone going. Make sure you have packed extra bags for rubbish and remember to leave no trace!

PACE

One of the biggest accommodations you will have to make when hiking with kids is that you will have to be flexible with pace. Be wary of making plans to meet anyone at any given time down the trail: you will most likely never make it, getting upset and frustrated in the (futile) process. Similarly, don't set time or distance targets – when hiking with kids time is not of the essence. Also keep in mind that *you* are most likely not to get a workout when hiking with little people. Well, not until you get to carry them . . .

SOME USEFUL EQUIPMENT

The right carrier for you:
Generally different carriers will work for different parents and different times. This is important because there is no right kind of carrier, and there is no one carrier that fits all tasks. Ultimately, you will need to find what works for you through a bit of savvy trial and error. (Your local Sling or Baby Carrier library might come in handy. Alternatively ask to borrow from friends for a weekend and try carriers out in real-life conditions before you commit.)

There is a dizzying array of carriers to choose from on the market that range from simple cloth wraparounds to more substantial versions that promise all the inconveniences of carrying a small caravan on your back. Baby carriers are either soft structured or external framed and before choosing the carrier for you, the best starting point is to consider what your needs are and what type of walking you mostly do. Not all carrier types fit both partners and who will be wearing the carrier the most is also an important consideration.

A whistle:
Give kids their own whistle, but make sure you teach them that it is for emergency use only. Although when hiking with kids you should choose suitable trails, a whistle can come in handy if at any point you become separated. When two of you are hiking with young kids it's best to have the children led by one adult and followed by a second one – keeping them in sight at all times. A head torch, for longer hikes, some sunscreen or waterproof clothing depending on the season and enough clothing are also good to have. Don't forget a basic first aid kit too!

GOING ON LONGER HIKES

For those who have mastered the day-hike, and are ready (and brave enough) to perhaps stray a bit further from home, as well as attempt a night or two away from all creature comforts, there's now research to suggest that there are great benefits to staying out in nature a little while longer.

In a study published in 2012, psychologists from the University of Kansas looked at how a multi-day hike affected creativity and problem solving tasks.[1] By looking at the fifty-six participants of a four-day hike programme and offering them a test designed to measure creativity and problem solving skills, the researchers found an incredible 50 per cent increase in higher-level cognitive function. They hypothesise that the sustained immersion in nature, as well as being away from technology, might be the reason for the increase. Despite several limitations in this particular study, including the small sample size, the theory of increased creativity in nature seems to be supported by anecdotal evidence too.

However, the multi-day hike poses a lot more challenges than the short jaunt I wrote about above. Pre-children, on one of our most memorable and challenging hikes up in the north of Greece, we encountered a father with his two young kids, aged seven and nine. I was very impressed by the two children, taking the incline and gravelly trail well into their stride and enduring quite a long way to reach a very remote mountain refuge, where we all stayed for the night. But I was also very impressed by their dad, who confidently led his kids up the steep mountain at a pace that suited them all, sustaining both his and their enthusiasm. We joined them for a brief section of the hike and chatted about their experience.

Firstly, it seemed that the kids had been hiking from an early age. Similar to our experience, introducing them to walking and hiking,

1 Atchley, R. A., Strayer, D. L., & Atchley, P. (2012). Creativity in the wild: Improving creative reasoning through immersion in natural settings. *PloS one*,*7*(12), e51474.

as well as other activities in natural environments, seemed to work better when started at an early age. Secondly, I was amazed at just how knowledgeable they were, both about their environment and its potential risks and pitfalls. They spoke to me about how best to tackle tricky mountain parts, like scree-covered slopes or wet areas, and schooled me on the importance of the right gear, and of trust and communication within the group. I was truly impressed by their heightened awareness of their surroundings, and their love of exploring new parts of the mountain. They chatted animatedly about their planned excursion for the next morning: a walk to the nearby Dragon-lake (a lake with a rare kind of newt that looks like a baby dragon). They were so excited that we decided to change our plans and join them!

LEAVE IT AS YOU FOUND IT (OR BETTER)

Going into nature is meant to be refreshing, even if your escape is a brief one. When you have children, you want them to explore and savour the outdoors. Coming across litter, or an act of vandalism, feels like an intrusion on your visit and makes the experience poorer (and can be distressing for children).

Connecting with nature doesn't only mean a walk in the woods. Nature can be found just outside your door even in urban environments. Small parks or communal gardens all provide opportunities to explore. In our garden, Joe and I had followed the patient progress of a female carder bee building her nests on a block of wood with several holes drilled in. One afternoon I came home to find that he had opened several of the nests in an effort 'for the babies to go to their mummy'. Whilst it was definitely a case of three steps forward and two steps back, it did allow for a relevant discussion of not disturbing animals and how we had damaged the bee's efforts. It is particularly difficult with young and inquisitive children, yet it is the best place to start. Visiting nature is exploring the big and the small – from our large and empty spaces to the expansive crowded world of mini-beasts wriggling under our feet.

The concept of leaving as little impact as possible on the areas that we visit need not be confined only to our national parks. It applies to everywhere.

- Value and appreciate the natural environment.
- Understand the impact of our activities and make correct choices on our actions.
- Respect other visitors.

ROAM AND TRAILS

Rules differ within the United Kingdom as to where you can walk freely and it is important to follow local signs and rules. You should follow paths unless wider access is available, such as on open country or registered common land. Leave gates, stiles and machinery as you find them, especially if you are on farm land.

Most green spaces will have well-maintained paths and they are there for a reason. They prevent soil erosion and damage to the local ecology. As exciting as it is to go off tramping through the bracken and explore off the trail, staying on a path preserves the ecology of the area. If you are walking with a large group of people it is better to space yourselves out along the path.

RESPECT FOR WILDLIFE

One of the main attractions when hiking or walking is the wildlife that you come across. While children may not be too excited by the early morning warble of a difficult to spot bird, larger animals like deer or cattle are always enthralling. Making too much noise or getting too close to wildlife is disturbing for them and can sometimes lead to young being abandoned. Be careful to keep a respectful distance from wild and farm animals during the mating and birthing seasons.

TO BUILD A FIRE OR NOT TO BUILD A FIRE

Lighting a wood fire is immensely satisfying, especially if you are out camping or you want to teach your children how to light a fire responsibly and safely. However, we can't all be like the great explorers, and bringing a camping stove is easier and less impactful on the environment. Fires that have got out of control cause immense damage to the local area, sometimes irreparably. Vigilance and being prepared are essential.

MIND YOUR ONES AND TWOS

Human faeces and urine can contaminate and spread a host of germs to natural water supplies if incorrectly disposed of. The best solution is to use a toilet if one is provided along the trail. The waste will be properly taken care of. The next best option is to bury it. Dig a hole away from the trail, campsite or any water source and cover up your business. There is nothing worse than finding little mounds of tissue paper when you have pets and curious children in tow. Bury your tissue paper or place it in a plastic bag and carry it out with you.

EVERY LITTLE BIT HELPS

Many walkers don't think twice about casting away an apple core, orange peel or banana skin on the grounds that it is biodegradable and they are in some small way helping to enrich the soil. Whilst the sentiment isn't at fault, banana and orange peels can take months to degrade: the John Muir Trust which manages Ben Nevis amongst other sites in the UK estimates that they can take up two years to degrade. Given the foot traffic that some popular areas receive you can see that these small well-intentioned efforts just take too long to degrade and a problem is created. Whilst it's not the same as throwing away a chocolate bar wrapper, we should endeavour to leave these areas in as good a condition as possible for the local ecosystems and other visitors. Parents of young children are no strangers to having reams of spare plastic bags with them to store an inevitable soiled item of clothing. Carry a plastic bag with you just in case you can do a good turn and pick up a small piece of litter. You can hold impromptu competitions to see who can pick up the most litter – within reason of course! Anything rusted or sharp should be left alone by young hands. This doesn't need to happen on every outing, but the positive modelling will have a great effect on your children and every little bit helps.

Volunteering is another option to make a difference. There are often opportunities for parents and children to help out in their local communities. The National Trust have a variety of programmes and are always looking for volunteers. Activities like cleaning a local beach (great for youngsters) or clearing walking paths (for those a little older) are a wonderful opportunity to make new friends and learn new skills, all the while experiencing the satisfaction of making a difference.

2 Boat races

A Year Outside Challenge
5 January
Weather: Wet, cold and windy

Third day of rain and now the wind has started too. I sit on the carpet in the living room, listening to the wind howling and the rain hitting the window panes horizontally. Normally I would have no intention of going outside on a day like this, but a challenge is a challenge.

'Fancy a walk up the mountain?' I ask, not expecting, or perhaps hoping against, a positive reply. Joe quietly leaves the room, only to return with his wellies on. Outside it is, then! I find all our bits of clothing and it takes me a good half hour to get the kids, and myself, dressed for this awful weather.

Yet once we are dressed it feels like the worst is over. The kids hop on the buggy and we climb the steep hill to the puddle – with so much rain Joe wants to see how much bigger it has got. Oliver watches, happily it seems, from under his woolly hat. I make a mental note to buy a better pair of gloves, as my fingers get colder and colder. Still, we spend a good hour outside, returning home wet, but with rosy cheeks and in a better mood for having been out. A.B.

This is an activity particularly suited to wet and windy days. You don't need a pond or access to the sea – a large puddle will do. We use just that: a puddle that collects rain water and can't be much deeper than an inch or two. The activity is simple and inspired by 'Poohsticks' – the game famously mentioned by A. A. Milne in *The House at Pooh Corner*, but without the need for running water or a bridge. In the traditional version of the game, for two or more players, the participants drop a stick from the upstream side of a bridge and then run and watch to see which stick appears first on the other side. Variations exist with arbitrary start- and finish-lines, as agreed by the players. Our version is simpler.

My three year old uses light sticks that he finds all around, although more sophisticated players and older children can make their very own boats, including sails, using natural materials from the surroundings. Once you have collected a few, you place them on the side of the puddle/pond/lake where the wind is coming from – let the children work this one out through trial and error.

Let go of your vessel and the race is on! The rules are simple: first boat to reach the end of the puddle wins. Watch as the boats travel across the water, aided only by the wind. When they reach their destination drop another and start all over again, or collect this one and take it back to the start. My boys are mesmerised by the travelling boats, and have a fun day out, despite the awful weather.

TAKING IT FURTHER

- Read *Stick Man* by Julia Donaldson and Axel Scheffler, for a first-person account of a stick-participant in a Poohsticks competition.
- Make a project of it. Go out and collect natural materials to make your own boats – large leaves, twigs and bits of bark work best, but let children improvise with anything that's at hand. Then go and set sail across the . . . puddles and see whose boat makes the journey.

3 Fun in the snow

A Year Outside Challenge
7 January
Weather: Snowy

The snow has fallen quietly through the night, leaving the landscape changed. The boys peer out at the white carpet covering the lawn, then get busy getting dressed. They haven't even had breakfast – Duncan agrees to take them out for a quick run-around in the garden, while I make porridge (and sneak some more coffee and a chocolate biscuit into me while they're not looking).

I then watch them through the window, squeals of delight reaching me as they play on the crunchy snow. It's not likely to last, so I make a plan to make the most of the white landscape before it disappears. A.B.

Depending on where you live, snow can be quite a novelty for your little ones. There are both positives and negatives to that. The advantage is that, most likely, if snow is a novelty your kids will be keen to go out and explore it. The downside is that you may not have the right clothes and equipment to keep them dry, warm and happy in the snow.

For us, although snowfall tends to be regular once or twice each winter, I find out that we are not quite prepared for it. Instead I pop several layers on the kids, and top them off with their rain-gear and wellies. That seems to do the trick. Ideally a snowsuit would have been preferable, but I resent the expense when we only get to play in snow twice a year (and they grow out of them within half a season!)

The snowfall has been generous, but not quite generous enough for us to make a shelter, despite the boys' effort. We do, however, have enough snow for a snowman. I throw the idea out there, but it seems both boys are more interested in simply exploring this cold substance that has changed the look of our back garden and the mountains all round.

Snow, like sand, water and clay, is one of the open-ended materials that present children with a whole world of opportunities. Children will usually let their imagination take over and play with it as they feel that day: one day it might be a snowball fight, the next building snow animals. I do, however, take the opportunity to give them some ideas. And just like that, we spend most of our morning building 'creatures' out of snow. Joe, our resident entomologist, is keen to make multi-legged insects, with antennae and round bodies, while Oliver is happy to pop sticks into my ready-made snow balls, making . . . sea urchins.

After a break, some hot apple juice and cinnamon, followed by a nap (for the younger members of the family) the early afternoon is spent using an old cardboard box to slide down the smallest of inclines. Both boys adore the makeshift tobogganing. I'm certain that if it snowed more often we would invest in a sledge, of sorts, but given the novelty, the cardboard box is just right, if a little soggy by the end of the hard play session.

TAKING IT FURTHER

- Snow is great for a host of arty activities – make a leaf and stone collage, or use food colouring in spray bottles to actually paint on snow.
- Forget about the boring snowman (although he too can be a starting point) and think of other creatures. The ones we made looked more like aliens than anything found on earth, but let children's imagination guide their artwork.
- Make sure they have a warm pair of gloves – there's nothing that will stop snow play quicker than cold hands (or feet).
- If you're far from home bring along a flask of hot chocolate or mulled apple juice to warm everyone up before you head home.

4 *Ice, ice baby*

A Year Outside Challenge

11 January

Weather: Icy, dry

The snow might have gone, but the cold weather certainly hasn't. It is cold, but dry, so we decide to dress well and head up the mountain. First call: Joe's puddle – he is keen to try one of the boats he has made with Duncan. Yet, when we get there and he places the boat on the puddle he finds that the water is rather . . . solid. Both boys are very intrigued – they use sticks to prod, they throw stones to explore this strange new 'thing' they have encountered and when they manage to break the ice enough for some water to come out they squeal. We pick up a little of the ice and they keep exploring. We return home and they spend the rest of the morning icicle hunting in the garden. In late afternoon we leave out a few of our own items to freeze, so we can inspect them in the morning. A.B.

Ice can be quite interesting for children – especially when they realise that it is water in a different form! Ice sheets, icicles and other forms of frozen creations can be tons of fun, although a good pair of gloves is a must again if you're going to enjoy them!

The challenge of 'delayed gratification', meaning the wait until the water they have placed outside has turned to ice, when planning to make icy creations can be tough for little ones, but if you can convince them to leave some full containers outside overnight you can have some great building blocks for a crystal fairy castle the next day.

TAKING IT FURTHER

- Use different containers to create icy shapes – we used our summer sand buckets, various plastic cups and bowls and half-filled balloons for a variety of shapes. Leave them out overnight and use them the next day as building blocks for houses, castles, etc. Use food colouring in the water for more colourful creations.

5 Den building

A Year Outside Challenge
2 February
Weather: Cold, dry

Sometimes the challenge is existential: you just cannot get motivated to head out. And sometimes, like today, you simply cannot get it together.

My toddler is still wearing no trousers two hours after getting out of bed, after he insisted that he wanted to practise wee-wees in the potty. The baby has crawled through said wee-wee that was lovingly deposited on the kitchen floor instead. Net effect = two kids with no pants on and mummy with the mop out.

The plan was to head out the door straight after breakfast, to seize the day, and enjoy today's winter sunshine. Yet, for lack of clean trousers, we are still in, train set out and some rather untimely Christmas music playing. I'm sure a movie is on the cards for later.

If I've learnt something in my (short) time as a mother it is that plans are not written in stone. I reassess the day's goal, from a walk to the nearest park, to a day in the back garden.

Three quarters of an hour later we are all dressed, and I feel drained. Plan B goes into action, to salvage the Year Outside Challenge: we head to our back garden. Today we are building a den! A.B.

I am yet to meet a child who does not enjoy den building. It is such a primal activity, such a natural instinct to provide shelter for yourself in the wild. It is also the lazy parent's favourite activity, it seems. Sign me up!

I am surprised, however, to find a host of research on dens. Norwegian childhood researcher Anne Trine Kjørholt links them to a separate 'children's culture', a world separate from that of adults.[1] This microcosm develops only in that special place, away from adults' eyes, where children are free to hide, play and keep secrets.

1 Kjørholt, A. T. (2003). 'Creating a Place to Belong': Girls' and Boys' Hut-building as a site for understanding discourses on childhood and generational relations in a Norwegian community. *Children's geographies, 1*(1), 261–79.

Another researcher, David Sobel, writes of the 'birth of self' in these special places,[1] and I can definitely see what he means, both in my very young boys playing outside, but also when observing older children building forts and dens. This idea of the den as the place where children grow 'themselves' seems to be supported by recent theories.

The den itself need not be fancy: it can be a pre-existing corner, slightly altered, to denote possession, it can be the little space between two bushes, or a more elaborate construction altogether. It is important, however, that the children build it themselves, and adults only intervene if they are asked. In this way children take ownership of the space – it becomes truly theirs![2]

I remember my own den building efforts – both indoors and outdoors – with such fondness and want to encourage my little ones to seek their private space. We start in the comfort of our garden, but eventually we will be building shelters in all sorts of places. Their first attempt at den building consists of asking me to cover the corner where two bushes meet with an old sheet – they then spend most of the morning going in and out, hiding from each other and occasionally fighting about who gets to sit inside.

1 Sobel, D. (1990). A place in the world: Adults' memories of childhood's special places. *Children's Environments Quarterly*, 5–12.
2 Kylin, M. (2003). Children's dens. *Children youth and environments, 13*(1), 30–55.

The next time, however, we get their slightly older friends to help us out!

Den building can take an hour or a year, and children are best left alone to complete the process as they see fit. It can happen in the wild, or in the safety of a back garden – we are lucky to have the latter option on this winter day. A local woodland or even a secluded spot at a local park can provide the right location. Make sure there are plenty of materials to hand: dead branches and big sticks, logs and fallen trees can all be used in the construction. In our case, we also use materials from inside – a broomstick, an old sheet and a rug are all incorporated into the design with gusto and flair. Other times find us building shelters in local woodland, with sticks of various sizes being our main building material.

TAKING IT FURTHER

- Read about famous dens in literature for inspiration: from Eeyore's house of sticks to Enid Blyton's *Hollow Tree House*. *Sally's Secret* by Shirley Hughes gives a heart-warming account of a little girl's secret place, that she also shares with her friends.
- For younger children who might struggle to make their own den I have found that a similar but easier project can be making a den for a favourite toy. A 'Shelter for Teddy' can be great fun and a starting activity for bigger and greater things.

6 *A walk in the dark*

A Year Outside Challenge

22 February

Weather: Wet, cold

Alexia sends me a text message at lunchtime informing me that we are all going for a walk. In the dark. At 6 p.m. It'll be fun, she says. Looking at the rain streaming down my classroom window I surmise that cabin fever has finally reached its tipping point and wonder if there is any way that I could work late today. It has been wet for the last few days, but as usual at this time of year, it is the darkness that gets to you. But later when I get home, the rain has broken to a fine drizzle and I brace myself for the scene that will greet me when I get inside. Instead of the expected scene of chaos where my wife is standing trussed up in loo paper sporting a new and engaging set of facial tics, an even eerier one greets me: with just a slight rustle of Gore-Tex and Macintosh fabric and whiff of rubber boots, there stands my little family waiting to go out. Head torches adorn their heads and whatever bits of reflective material Alexia could find have been taped to our children. The sheer excitement in Joe's face at the possibility of going out after the sun has set shows she might have been right all along: this does look like it will be fun. D.B.

Something magical happens each and every evening. The normal, the mundane, the simple walk round the block takes on a completely different essence when it's in the dark. Everything is different at night, and the closer you are to nature the more things change. You can hear different bird calls, different shadows are cast, and if you are animal spotting, you are more likely to see that elusive fox, or a low swooping owl.

As we set off on our first walk I notice just how much quieter everything seems. It is an overcast night, so no stargazing for us. Joe is nonetheless singing 'Twinkle twinkle little star' and spends a big part of our walk looking up, in an effort to spot the little star, or a rare-for-him glimpse of the moon.

We are being led by our head torches – both boys love the novelty and I remember what it is about this time of the evening that I love. Although we take our normal walk, staying on the familiar roads around our house, nothing is familiar: it is suddenly all so novel and strange. We spend some of the time singing, but then we also make a point of walking in silence too – trying to listen out for all the night-time creatures.

For older kids a night-time walk does not have to happen at dusk, but can take place at any point in the night, or just before dawn. Nor do you have to stay on the well-trodden paths you usually take: a walk in the woods can be exhilarating and can become a real adventure, involving maps and treasure hunts. Let your imagination run wild and look at how things are different when the light of day is gone. Make sure you stay safe by carrying a spare torch and batteries, as well as a charged mobile phone for any emergencies.

TAKING IT FURTHER

- Read about the creatures of the night – what animals are you likely to encounter?
- For young kids (up to four years old) read *Owl Babies*, by Martin Waddell and Patrick Benson. The tale of three young owls who wait for their mummy to come back in the dark will warm hearts and should pique the young reader's interest about creatures of the night.
- For older kids (aged five to nine) a brilliant book that will give them an insight into the differences between day and night is *The Owl Who Was Afraid of the Dark*, by Jill Tomlinson. Explore night-time practices, animals and the beauty of the dark by reading it as you make your small outings into the dark.
- Upper primary children might prefer a more scientific look into night-time creatures. Non-fiction books, such as *100 Facts Nocturnal Animals* by Camilla de la Bedoyere, and websites, such as BBC Nature, can give you an idea of what to look for in your back garden, your neighbourhood or further afield.

7 Do you speak 'nature'?

A Year Outside Challenge

3 March

Weather: Cold and cloudy, light drizzle

On this cloudy morning, despite the light rain, we are enjoying looking for some flowers for Joe to take home for our special guest this evening – his godmother is coming to visit.

A rather untimely spring has arrived, it seems, and our almost daily walks up on the mountain have been taken over by the search for wild flowers. Joe is most keen to find little colourful buds and point them out to me. Sometimes he picks a bunch to take home (but I make sure he doesn't pick anything rare) and then he looks at it for hours, inspecting each and every flower, its stalk, its leaves and petals, its stamens and the occasional sprinkling of golden pollen.

I am a firm believer in calling things by their proper names, including plants and flowers, although I'm by no means an expert in taxonomy. But when Joe picks up a flower, holds it towards me and informs me proudly that he has found a crocus, I swell with pride. A.B.

The power of language is huge. It shapes our perceptions, and provides a medium for describing the contents of our conscious experience.[1] We humans tend to name all the things that are important to us. That's why people who are really into cars know all their brands and models (and why, half the time I still tell people that my car is 'red' when they ask me what type I have) and that's why naturalists, like Carl Linnaeus, came up with a special classification system to name all plants and animals.

I want to show my sons that nature, its plants and animals, matter to me too. Although when I take stock of the names that I do know they seem to cover a rather large percentage of our local flora, I am still keen to know more. Joe is amazed by the fact that each flower, each grass and bush has its own name – just like each person does. He loves the idea that he can be precise in his communication with me and on top of that I feel that he is picking up my enthusiasm for the subject.

Learning the names of the most common flowers, trees and insects around us used to be a rather organic process. I remember learning about wild herbs, like thyme and oregano, as we picked them as kids with my parents. I also remember learning to identify stinging nettles and thorny bushes rather quickly! Pines were all around, and cypresses were what was used as windbreakers and all around cemeteries in the nature of my childhood. Aspen tree bark was covered with eyes (I now know that in some places they

1 Klemfuss, N., Prinzmetal, W., & Ivry, R. B. (2012). How does language change perception: a cautionary note. *Frontiers in psychology, 3*, 78.

call it 'eyeball tree'), while the bark of eucalyptus trees could be peeled off, leaving behind lovely swirly patterns on the trunk.

By talking to my sons using the names of the trees and flowers around us I am passing on several messages to them. First of all, I pass on what I feel is important cultural knowledge. Nowadays kids are more likely to be able to identify brand names and logos than name three or four local plants. Secondly, I want my children to feel at home in the natural environment, I want them to feel like they are amongst friends, and the first step towards this was to teach them some of the names of the plants all around us. Finally, I want to show my kids that I value the diverse nature we inhabit, that I think it important enough to name it. Just as other children can tell a Peugeot from a Volkswagen, or Nike from Adidas, it is important for me that my children can tell daisies from chamomile (clue: they have very different leaves).

It doesn't come easy, I have to do a little bit of research before I can confidently tell a dandelion from a yellow hawkweed, but I let Joe know that I don't know very much and that he can help me too. I am delighted when he starts calling spring flowers by their names, feeling comfortable and simply at home in the nature that surrounds us.

TAKING IT FURTHER

- Depending on where you live, you and your child can visit the local botanical gardens to learn more about your local plants, as well as more exotic ones. If you are in London, Kew Gardens offer unrivalled diversity, but other cities, especially those with universities, tend to have botanical gardens ranging from the grand and old, like the Royal Botanic Garden Edinburgh, to the smaller but equally interesting. Oxford is home to the oldest botanical garden and arboretum in the UK.

- For older children the identification process can become quite a challenge by using botanical keys like the one available online by the Botanical Society of Britain and Ireland.
- A botanical sketchbook can be a worthwhile project for older children too. There are even guides available on how to keep one. For younger kids, drying and keeping flowers can offer a chance at starting a collection. Frame some and give them as gifts, or keep them and leaf through them to remind yourself of your jaunts into local nature.

8 *Stone throwing*

A Year Outside Challenge
5 March
Weather: Cold, overcast

It's a cold dark morning and I have had to drive a good twenty miles to the nearest post office depot to pick up a parcel. I tell myself that it is the price we have to pay for living in the mountains, and count my blessings, but the flat, grey sky is threatening us with rain and I feel rather uninspired.

The children have fallen asleep in the back, the long drive working its magic. I pull over into a car park by the beach and close my eyes too. I can hear seagulls in the background, but not for long, the sleepless nights have taken their toll and I'm asleep in no time.

I awake to a baby blowing raspberries in the back. Not too long afterwards Joe wakes up and, though disorientated, is excited to see the sea.

A few minutes later we are on the pebbly beach, looking at the unusually calm sea. Oliver is fascinated by the seagulls, but Joe seems to have discovered the art of stone throwing. He weighs the stone in his hand first, enjoying the roundness of the sea-smoothed rock, and then he sends it up into the air, watching carefully as it breaks the perfect, almost oily, surface of the sea. The ripples are mesmerising for all of us and we watch them until they fade. A.B.

There is something very primal about pebble throwing. Put any child, or adult for that matter, by a body of water and you'll see them pick up and throw pebbles, just for fun. Tossing pebbles, stones or rocks into bodies of water seems to have a deeper meaning in some traditions. In Celtic lore, pebble tossing is a wedding tradition that is sometimes still observed. The idea is that a physical object, like a pebble or stone, anchors a thought, wish or prayer. It is then tossed into a nearby body of water. The symbolism of the stone – as well as water, an element linked to the spirit, but also to flow, travel and change – is strong and goes back centuries.

Similar traditions of throwing pebbles or coins into wells and fountains exist in other cultures around the world. I still remember the two coins (and the wishes that went with them) that my husband and I threw into the Trevi fountain on our first visit to Rome!

Yet put two or more children on a beach or riverside and suddenly pebble throwing can become quite competitive: who can throw the furthest, or who can find the biggest stone. I can see Joe truly getting into the spirit of pebble throwing – really straining as he tosses the pebbles into the calm water.

You don't even need a beach to have fun throwing stones – on our daily walk we meet a puddle of water about big as a car and as shallow as they get, and yet Joe always stops, throws a few pebbles in and watches the ripples carefully. I think there is something deeply symbolic about the way the ripples spread out from the pebble and I can see he loves to see the effect his action has even on this small body of water.

STONE SKIMMING

Stone skimming (UK) or stone skipping (US), ducks and drakes, stone skiffing, or frog jumps – whatever you call it, it seems to be a widespread activity that attracts both children and grown-ups. It has a rich history, claimed by some to go back to the ancient Greeks. There are championships, both for number of jumps and distance, as well as an official Guinness record. The record of thirty-eight 'jumps' has been unbeatable for over twenty years (it goes back to 1992).

There seems to be both an art and a science to stone skimming. In the book *The Art of Stone Skipping and Other Fun Old-Time Games: Stoopball, Jacks, String Games, Coin Flipping, Line Baseball, Jump Rope, and More* author and mum of three J. J. Ferrer devotes two full pages to the description of this art. On the other hand, physicist Lyderic Bocquet has written several articles, published in prestigious journals, such as the *American Journal of Physics*[1] exploring the fairly complex – at least to the untrained physicist, judging by the amount of formulae involved – process of the successful stone skim. A follow-up article in *Nature*[2] will tell you all about the secrets of successfully launching your flat rock onto the water's surface.

1 Bocquet, L. (2003). The physics of stone skipping. *American journal of physics, 71*(2), 150–5.
2 Clanet, C., Hersen, F., & Bocquet, L. (2004). Secrets of successful stone-skipping. *Nature, 427*(6969), 29–9.

However, you don't need a physics degree to enjoy the process of stone skimming and I have many fond memories of spending hours not just attempting to get the most jumps, but on the search for the right stone. Anyone who has ever enjoyed this pastime will empirically know that the best stones are flat and rather circular, that speed and angle are important, and that just the right flick is needed to give the stone a bit of spin.

TAKING IT FURTHER

- There are a number of more official games, mostly played outdoors, that are a natural progression from the pebble throw. A lot of these will be attractive to older children and young teens. The Italian *bocce*, traditionally played on natural soil, is said to originate from Ancient Rome and has moved – 'carried' by Italian migrants – all around the globe. Equally, the French *boules*, British bowls and the Croatian *boćanje* are all usually played on natural soil or lawn.

SPRING

9 Springwatch

A Year Outside Challenge

21 March (Vernal Equinox)

Weather: Cool but dry

'The daffodils are out,' shouts Joe from the garden, or something to the same effect. I am in the kitchen, trying to get some precious sips of coffee down me before the start of the day. The boys, as they have been doing more and more recently, seem as keen as the dogs are to get out in the morning, and usually follow our trusty canines into the garden first thing, and stay there for hours, in their pyjamas and coats, on the days when it's not wet.

I join them to see what Joe is so excited about and note the daffodils are now in full bloom. We have watched them for days, the green buds swelling, then slowly raising their heads, and then the yellow petals unfolding, one at a time, to end up standing proud and open, greeting the weak spring sun. Today it truly feels like spring. A.B.

Spring is a magical time of year. The rebirth of nature, after a long winter, is a miracle to behold, and becomes more so when shared with young children for whom it is a new experience. I have been talking to Joe a lot about the seasons, making sure I link them with what has been going on in our lives. The more time we spend in nature, of course, the more relevant seasonal change becomes.

On top of that we can all learn to attune our senses to the seasonal changes happening around us, we can approach the world with a sense of wonder for our constantly changing surroundings, and who better to lead us into this than children. I realised this the first time that Joe encountered snow, at the age of about eighteen months. He had a playfulness and at the same time a little apprehension at this fluffy white substance that appeared out of nowhere, fell from the sky, felt cold to the touch and quickly melted on contact with his skin. He looked at me quizzically, then continued to explore the unexpected change to our back garden. After it was all covered in snow we went out. I remember his excitement at the *crunching sound* the packed snow made under his wellington boots!

Similarly, the closer we get to nature this spring the more Joe notices the changes. I am amazed at how perceptive he is even when it comes to minor and gradual changes: to leaves coming out in trees, to bulbs flowering, to the grass getting greener or growing faster.

With older children seasonal changes can be documented in a more systematic way. You can keep a calendar for first sightings (first time you see a ladybird, a certain species of butterfly, or the first budburst and leaf of a specific type of tree).

TAKING IT FURTHER

- Join the Woodland Trust (link at the end) for a more formal approach to springwatch, as well as exciting information on what to look for.
- Keep a photo diary, or – with older children – make your own time-lapse movie by taking a picture a day.

10 Sand play

A Year Outside Challenge
28 March
Weather: Cold and overcast, mainly dry

The boys are playing in the garden and I can barely hear them. I am inside spring cleaning, literally and figuratively. I am putting some of our winter shoes and boots away, making room for flip-flops and plimsolls. I shake each pair out, fearing the centipedes that love to build their home in the darkness of our boots, as I have experienced one too many times. As I shake out Oliver's blue and red stripy wellies a stream of sand falls out. In fact, the more I shake, the more sand seems to appear. It takes me back to a few weekends ago, when the boys seemed to spend most of their day in a sand pit: building, cooking, sifting, pouring. A.B.

As a primary school teacher I was always amazed by the fascination that sand play held for certain children. Some kids used to love playing in the sand pit, day in day out. And it wasn't just for the little ones either – there were children as old as ten who would rather spend some time there, digging and building, than running or playing hide-and-seek. Unfortunately, at most schools, the sand pit is only available to the early years' classroom, leaving valuable exploration and play inaccessible for older children.

Sand is an excellent open-ended resource. To put it simply, like water and unlike many modern toys, there is no right or wrong way to use sand. Children can be truly creative and play in developmentally appropriate ways. For example, younger children will often play alone, building structures, while older children will construct elaborate stories that require advanced social skills, imagination and creativity.

Moreover, sand play can develop both gross and fine motor skills. Digging, carrying and pushing sand around work on gross motor skills, while other activities, like sifting, drawing on sand and pouring sand through one's hands can develop finer skills. Importantly, sand offers a novel sensory experience for kids, through the feeling and manipulating of the sand itself, as well as various 'tools' the child might use, which include sticks, stones and shells, as well as man-made objects like rakes, buckets and spades.

I am keen to let my sons play and explore the medium of sand. Access to sand pits was unfortunately limited for us and, while the beach presented us with one possibility, Duncan and I discussed the idea of building a sand pit at home, in our small back garden.

TAKING IT FURTHER

- If you have the space, and the inclination, making a sand pit in your own back garden can provide hours of fun (for the children, mostly). Alternatively, a sand and water table, available from most toy stores, can be used in the smallest of outdoor spaces, including balconies or paved yards.

HOW TO MAKE A SAND PIT

Surprisingly there are a plethora of designs for keeping a cubic metre or two of sand enclosed in a wooden casing. Perhaps understandable given how successfully a sand pit can keep a child interested for hours, and with dads dying to put their tools to use.

Duncan spent hours planing and sanding thick planks of wood that he had found. On reflection he probably felt that the amount of effort he put into it would translate into the amount of enjoyment the children would have. The children were oblivious to the wood joining methods he used and a great amount of joy was to be had in throwing the sand out of the pit.

So, the lessons learnt are:

- Don't overthink the construction. Go for safe, sturdy and uncomplicated.
- Always have a cover for the sand pit. The main reason for needing a cover is to keep the sand clean. Cats will happily jump on the opportunity to use this convenient and spacious litter box. Plastic covers that do not let the air in can keep the sand damp and can create a happy haven for frogs. Using a cover made from shade netting will allow the rain to wash the sand, keeping it clean. Provided you have good drainage, this shouldn't be a problem.

11 *Fewer playthings, more play*

A Year Outside Challenge

29 March

Weather: Warm(ish) and sunny

It is one of the most beautiful spring mornings we've had so far, and Joe, Oliver and I have met some friends at a local woodland. I have volunteered to lead the kids on an adventure into the forest, and as we come into a clearing, bathed in sunlight, I am excited that the children are no longer following me but have spread all around me. Some are climbing a fallen tree, some have found sticks and are prodding them into the soil, soft from last night's rain. Joe and a friend are watching a long line of ants, marching out of their home. Oliver is pushing twigs into a pine cone. I am happy to sit back and watch them explore.

And then something happens. One of the mums brings out a bag of toys, cars and Playmobil people, and places it in the middle of the clearing! I am amazed at the speed that the children leave what they are doing and flock to the bag. In no time they have taken the toys, and have once more spread about the clearing. Only this time they are not playing together. They each have a car and limit themselves to making 'car noises' broom-brooming their way round. Very little interaction is now taking place, apart from a little squabble over a red formula 1 car, which is only resolved after parental intervention. I feel the forest adventure has come to a swift and undeserved end. A.B.

The relationship between toys and play is a complicated one, and it seems that it is directly linked with the type of toys we are referring to. Simple, open-ended toys, like empty boxes, wooden blocks or cardboard tubes seem to elicit more vigorous and creative play than dolls with fixed expressions, plastic phones that light up and electronics.

Allowing kids to put their own meaning on their playthings, to truly explore the possibilities of each item, as well as engage in imaginative and creative play, means that often we have to make the right toys available to them. When in nature, that becomes easier than we think: leaving kids to find their own playthings, including, but not limited to, sticks and twigs, leaves and blossom, shells and rocks of different sizes, pine cones and many other natural 'toys' that kids find, explore and play with.

Similarly, the number of toys that children are presented with can also affect both the way they play, but also whether they truly engage with them or not. In general, when children are in a new situation, or come into contact with a new medium (e.g water, foam, sand) or toy, they tend to go through an initial exploration period, before they begin to play.[1] The more toys children have available to play with, the more likely they are to actually spend their time exploring: that is, finding out what a toy can do and what they can do with the toy, and the less time spent actually playing with something, actively engaging and creating meaning and stories.

I believe bringing toys into natural surroundings takes away from the splendid opportunities provided by the

1 Vandenberg, B. (1984). Developmental Features of Exploration. *Developmental Psychology*, 20, 3–8.

surroundings themselves. They take over and grab children's attention away from exploration, and they can often dictate how the children engage with their environment, as well as with each other.

Even away from natural environments, in the classroom, taking toys away can help children find creative solutions, play more with each other and even moderate behaviour. In a fascinating study that took place in Germany, dubbed 'The Toy-Free Kindergarten' (*Der Spielzeugfreie Kindergarten*),[1] two social workers did just what the title suggests. They took away all the toys, allowed for a less structured day for the kids . . . then sat back and watched. The results were definitely interesting.

At first children were at a loss on what to do. All their toys had been taken away and only the furniture was left: chairs and tables, and a few blankets. That's right: no toy cars, no dolls and no crayons and paper, either! They looked around at each other, then looked at the empty room. In the next few days, and for several weeks, the children started playing with the items that were available: they made caves out of the chairs and blankets, they took out the drawers from the chests in the room and used them to construct their own meaning, pretending they were walls, or plates, or carts.

1 http://www.spielzeugfreierkindergarten.de/pdf/englisch.pdf accessed 2 April 2016

Their games became a lot more involved, the children socialised better and became creative in their approach to play. Several weeks in they started finding ways to 'make' their own playthings – bringing in wooden planks and tools from home. With the help of their teachers they built several constructions, including a mill.

I love reading about this and spend days discussing it with my husband, yet there is a part of me that is hesitant to remove our sons' toys. A reason for that is that in our culture toys are equated with play, and play, in turn, is the *raison d'être* of childhood. And so, in a small part of my mind, I am worried that by removing toys, I am somehow taking something away from my children, something that is rightfully theirs.

Yet, after a horrid week of constant toy taking and squabbling, often ending in tears, my husband makes the brave move, while I am at work. I get a message on my phone, a picture, showing the two boys playing happily. I am amazed – then the text comes: 'Took all toys away. Boys playing happily outside together. Interesting.'

The trend continues for the rest of the week. Without toy cars to push down the little bump of a hill in our garden, the boys are using their own bodies to roll down the hill, squeals of laughter filling the yard. They don't seem to miss their toys for one second, instead they are busy playing hide-and-seek, collecting pine cones and cooking with them, making mud soup and watching the bugs in the garden. I watch them with joy, but also with a deep sense of relief that they are no longer fighting over the yellow digger! It's not all plain sailing: they do occasionally get bored, or decide that they both want the very same twig, at the same time. But our days in the garden are calmer, more creative and the kids are interacting more positively.

TAKING IT FURTHER

- If your kids are playing within your own space (garden) or they go somewhere regularly, make sure there are enough open-ended playthings around, some natural, some not. A few pine cones, sticks and rocks, even cardboard boxes, planks and car tyres can be used.
- If you are visiting natural spaces, like woodlands or beaches, have a look at all the available resources that can be used to make things or play with. Sticks and stones, sand and mud, logs and tree trunks can all make great, open-ended playthings.
- Fiona Danks and Jo Schofield's *The Stick Book: Loads of Things You Can Make or Do with a Stick* can definitely provide inspiration for the countless uses of a stick out in nature.

12 *Little farmers – growing our own vegetables*

A Year Outside Challenge

10 April

Weather: Warm(ish) and sunny

I really hope the neighbours aren't watching. I am in that tired fog that only new parents know, the grey kind that swirls around your ankles. I am wearing my old dressing gown, I can't remember if I have tied it closed or not. I am upright and waiting for my coffee to dissipate the fog so that I can have a clearer idea of what Joe and Oliver are doing. Last night was rough, and I like to think that I have rather gallantly taken both kids out of the house so Alexia can get a little sleep but deep down I know it is fear of my tired and grumpy wife. I recalled the scene from Legends of the Fall *rather too vividly where Brad Pitt gets mauled by the bear and I imagined the same fate could await me with my overtired wife. And so we escape the house for the safety of the vegetable patch. I am tired. The latest thing for the boys is to turn on the tap and water everything. Oliver is naked, well the bottom half of him. When and where the nappy went I am not too sure. The fog parts slightly and I realise that the boys are happily washing away the radish seeds we planted a few days ago. Maybe we are onto something here. Alexia gets some much-needed peace and quiet and the boys are engaged and getting their hands dirty. I'll need to go to the garden centre again. D.B.*

Keeping your children involved with the growth cycle from the watering can to the table is a sure way to ensure excitement in the vegetables that end up on their plate. Using a combination of pot plants and raised beds is an excellent way to involve your children in growing fruits and vegetables, and are an efficient use of space.

Raised beds have several advantages. They can be placed on top of any surface and so give you freedom in planning your layout. The extra height means it is easier on your back and also creates a barrier to children tramping through your vegetable bed. By bringing the plants to near eye level, the growth process becomes much more exciting for children and it makes it easier for them to spot slugs and snails! Raised beds have been found to be more productive than conventional beds as you can plant your vegetables closer together because you don't need to leave space to walk between rows of plants. Moreover, because your plants are closer together, it is harder for weeds to take root in bare shaded soil. More productive and less weeding – what's not to love?

Raised beds also give you a lot of freedom in construction, and they are easy to attach a trellis to for climbing plants as well as to secure hoops for shade netting. They also have improved drainage. This does mean that you need to take care in summer that the bed doesn't dry out, but it also means they will be warmer in spring and you can get a head start on your planting. Although they are not difficult to build, be aware they take a surprising amount of soil and compost to fill – a simple 2m × 1m × 20cm bed requires around half a cubic metre of soil.

MATERIALS NEEDED

Most home hardware stores will sell you either plastic ready-formed sheets for raised-bed gardening, or more aesthetically pleasing wood kits. The advantage of building your own is that you can design the bed to the dimensions that best suit your space. Scaffold boarding is a good, sturdy and affordable option for wood. Heat-treated wood too is easily available; it's chemical free and can last for years. This saves you having to treat your wood with varnish or protective oils.

CONSTRUCTING YOUR RAISED BED

Using corner posts will give your construction added strength. When attaching the sides, drill pilot holes one size smaller than the screws you are using (this makes the job easier and prevents shearing and the possibility of the wood splitting). Another option, easier still, is to use steel brackets to secure your corners. Fill the bed with nutrient rich compost and soil and you shouldn't have to use fertiliser.

WHAT AND HOW TO PLANT

- Plant vegetables that your children like. There is no point growing vegetables that they are not interested in until you can broaden their tastes.
- Choose plants that are interesting to watch grow. That might sound silly, but radishes and carrots are a mystery to children until they come out of the ground. Tomatoes, peppers and cucumbers are far more interesting to monitor

progress with as they flower, bud, swell, ripen and change colour.

- Plant in order of height. The only reason I list this is that it has worked for us! Arrange your plants so that the children can see what is going on from shortest to tallest. It will go a long way to keeping their interest. For example, closest to the edge of the container you could plant strawberries, basil, lettuce, carrots. A row back could be chard and then your taller plants, tomatoes, peppers, with sweet peas in the middle as they can be trained upwards. If you have the space, sweetcorn and sunflowers are always captivating to youngsters.
- You can keep your children involved and your dinners healthy all year round. In early spring and late summer you can plant the semi-hardy and hardy vegetables that can tolerate the cold. Radish, spinach and cauliflower do well. After the threat of frost, in late spring you can start on the vegetables that thrive on warmer weather. Tomatoes, cucumbers, peppers and pumpkins enjoy the sun and are in my opinion the more interesting fruits to grow! Your local garden centre will stock a variety of tasty vegetables at the right planting time.

PLANTING IN POTS

Pots are a great alternative or a handy supplement to raised beds. Assigning the responsibility of a pot to a child always works, especially if you have more than one child. You have a greater choice of locations with pots and you can move them around if you are trying to chase, or even hide them from the sun! Perennial herbs such as rosemary, thyme and oregano require little management and are best placed close to the kitchen. Window ledges and balconies are often ideal spaces to be used for those.

Locate your pots against a wall or fence away from cold drying winds. Because potted plants won't have access to underground moisture, consistent watering is vital. Make sure your pots have good drainage, use good quality potting compost and don't use garden soil. You will most likely need to top up your potting compost in a few months and fertilise. Check your soil mix to check whether it has short term or slow-release fertiliser.

TAKING IT FURTHER

- Not only will your new vegetable garden be a source of interest to your children, it will also pique the attention of birds. As much as we want to encourage birdlife, it is a little heartbreaking to watch a strawberry ripen for days and just before picking, see it snapped up by a bird! As a fun activity to protect your fruit and vegetables, make paper or plastic windmills, scarecrows or stick in poles with streamers attached, all to whizz and whirr and keep the birds away.

13 The birds . . .

A Year Outside Challenge

19 April

Weather: Cool, breezy

I am reliably informed, by other parents, that not all children like to wake up at the crack of dawn. My kids, however, have not received that memo . . . With mornings becoming lighter as spring establishes itself, the boys start waking up earlier and earlier. I struggle to keep up at first, and complain bitterly, then hit the coffee hard to fuel the morning. But then one day, after an early morning wake-up, while Joe, Oliver and I are sitting on the grass, each sipping our beverage of choice (coffee for me, milk for the boys) we all notice the most glorious morning chorus.
Then a strange thing happens: once we have noticed it, it becomes deafening. I wonder how we have managed to ignore it all this time. And the next day, we can't. I lie in my bed, early in the morning, and let the dawn chorus gently wake me up. I may still need that coffee, but I can definitely think of worse ways to wake up! A.B.

THE DAWN CHORUS

It seems that spring is the best season for the dawn chorus, and that the main reasons for birds to sing so much so early is to defend breeding territory, as well as to attract a mate. A study in the tropical forests of Ecuador established that certain types of birds – those that nest higher up and those that have bigger eyes – tend to start singing earliest each morning.[1] I am guessing sensitivity to sunlight is connected to that.

In the UK the early morning chorus can start even before dawn, with some species starting to pipe up well before day break.[2] Robins, wrens and song thrushes tend to start first, followed by other 'late risers'. Surprisingly, the well-known 'cock-a-doodle-doo' that we associate with early mornings is often more to do with defending of property, or wooing of a hen, than the start of the day. Not only that, but one study found that even in a darkened room, roosters know when it's morning and time their crowing appropriately, due to their circadian rhythm (so it's not the morning light itself that determines when the cockerel crows!).[3]

I am excited to find out that there is an annual International Dawn Chorus Day, celebrated each year on the first Sunday of May. Events are organised for listening to and recording the dawn chorus across the world, from the Caribbean to Antarctica.[4] I'm certainly looking forward to the next International Dawn Chorus Day and wonder if I should organise my own event, right here in

1 Jamieson, B. G. M. (2007). *Pt. B: Sexual selection: behavior: conservation: embryology: genetics* (Vol. 6). Enfield, NH [etc.]: Science Publishers.
2 http://www.bl.uk/listentonature/specialinterestlang/langofbirds3.html accessed 14 April 2016
3 Shimmura, T., & Yoshimura, T. (2013). Circadian clock determines the timing of rooster crowing.*Current biology, 23*(6), R231–R233.
4 http://idcd.info/idcd/ accessed 14 April 2016

our back garden. I wonder if anyone would attend at that time in the morning . . . maybe if cake is offered, and coffee on tap!

BIRD FEEDERS

In 2009, while living in Greece our house was nearly destroyed by an out of control wildfire. The next morning when returning to the house we were relieved to find the house hadn't suffered substantial damage, but every tree and shrub had been scorched. Aside from the charred smell, the most striking thing was the absence of noise. Neither a bee buzzed nor a bird called. Just silence. As dead tree roots were dug up and new saplings planted, one of the goals was to entice birdlife back to the garden.

Loss of habitat is the greatest threat to the birds and the bees across the UK.[1] Feeding birds is an incredibly popular pastime in Britain, and the Royal Society for the Protection of Birds (RSPB) estimates that more than half of all adults feed birds. There are a great many different types of feed and different types of feeder. Auxiliary feeding does not provide all the required nutrients of a wild diet; nevertheless your efforts are of great assistance to birds. When starting out, it is best to know which species you would like to assist and which are the local bird species. Different seeds, grains and nuts are beneficial to different types of birds. For

1 Oliver, T. H., Isaac, N. J., August, T. A., Woodcock, B. A., Roy, D. B., & Bullock, J. M. (2015). Declining resilience of ecosystem functions under biodiversity loss. *Nature communications*, *6*.

example, larger birds such as pigeons and doves enjoy wheat and barley and can often chase away smaller birds if you mix those grains with other bird feed. Deciding to feed birds is an exciting year round activity and you can even use some kitchen scraps! Every now and then a new species of bird is spotted and the boys are keen to save any scraps or seed toppings that are left behind from a finished loaf of bread.

Bird feeders provide an opportunity to bring a variety of species into your garden. You can help birds when there are food shortages or during periods of severe weather and at the same time open up the exciting world of birds to your children. What you put out to feed changes throughout the year.

SUMMER AND SPRING FEEDING

Scraps of fruit, clean eggshells to help with calcium replacement and some nesting materials can be of help.

WINTER FEEDING

Nuts and grains with high fat content such as peanuts, black sunflower and nyjer seeds. Homemade fat balls (lard with a variety of ingredients).

As with bird feed, there are a wide range of feeders from which you can choose what to put in your garden. Worthy charities like the RSPB are excellent places to start. For the DIY enthusiast the sky's the limit in terms of what you can make. Designs range from reusing wine bottles and old crockery to avian Swiss-style chalets.

BIRD BATHS

Bird baths have been another source of great excitement for the children. Spotting a bird splashing itself in the garden always leads to yells of excitement from the boys and a wet and hasty departure for the bird. Bird baths will attract more birds than a feeder will as insectivorous birds such as robins and wagtails won't visit most feeders, but a freshwater bath is always appealing and all birds need to drink.

Bird baths need:

- Clean water.
- A shallow depth of 5–8 centimetres.
- Sides that have enough texture for birds to grip.
- To be sited away from shrubs that cats can hide in.

Elevated bird baths are the best option as they are easier to watch from the house, and they give the birds a chance to see a predator coming.

TERRACOTTA POT SAUCER BIRD BATH

Place a terracotta plant pot saucer on top of an upright log or stump, or on a large overturned terracotta pot or even a stack of pots. You can experiment placing your pots end-to-end or if you prefer a tapering effect you can stack them upside down in decreasing sizes. For added stability and especially if you have small children about, it is best to secure the pots to each other either with glue or by running a threaded rod with a washer and nut through the pots.

Remember, mosquitos love standing water so it is best to tip out the water regularly to avoid larvae hatching.

14 . . . and the bees

A Year Outside Challenge
3 May
Weather: Warm(ish) and sunny

I am sitting in the garden, feeling immensely pleased with myself. I have just got back from my first solo inspection of my new beehive. It couldn't have gone better really – so well in fact that I was fairly sure I heard the ever patient and dulcet vowels of David Attenborough as I inspected each form of bee busily doing its thing. And I haven't been stung. I know I will be, but as a new beekeeper I still see this as a success. To say that I have been fascinated by bees for a while is an understatement, and despite Alexia's practical misgivings she eventually gave in, reasoning that as far as mid-life crises go, this is a fairly innocuous one.

It is spring and the garden is alive. I ponder if any of the bees buzzing around are 'mine'. Improbable, but just possible, as my apiary is in a field not too far away. Joe is running around pointing to any bee he sees as 'daddy's bee'. Oliver for his part is still too young and finds de-leafing anything he can reach a most diverting activity. He is our very own household version of Agent Orange on anything knee high. Every now and then I see a bumblebee or some unknown sort of bee. Banded hoverfly? I really don't know. I wonder why I never noticed them last year. I will visit the garden centre later this afternoon. I want to make the garden a bit more bee friendly, and if it helps some of 'my bees' then so much the better. D.B.

Our small garden used to be neatly tended with closely cut grass, tidily clipped hedges and ornamental flowers in pleasing locations. A little too clinical. That all changed once Duncan took up beekeeping. Season by season the garden has changed. New flower beds and shrubs have encroached on the once rectangular lawn area. Not a walk in the neighbourhood goes by without Duncan coming back with a new idea or a new plant to fit into the garden. In many ways the garden has been 're-wilded' and is now energetically abuzz. Joe and Oliver are old enough to understand that the bees provide the honey on their toast, and ever keen to keep that tenuous link intact have left the flower beds largely untrespassed.

According to the National Ecosystem Assessment (NEA), domestic gardens comprise 18 per cent of the urban landscape in the UK. That is an awfully large area that with a relatively small effort could be of great assistance to pollinators. There is growing awareness of the difficulties faced by the European honeybee. Loss of habitat, climate change, disease and the threat of neonicotinoids are all threatening this helpful insect's future. But it is not alone – in Britain there are more than two hundred and twenty species of solitary bee and twenty-four species of bumblebee, all of which are excellent pollinators and can keep your garden healthy.

TAKING IT FURTHER

- Involving children in an active garden is all part of the fun. Bumblebee spotting doesn't require an anorak and you can keep track of the species that visit your garden. For further help there is the 'Bumblebees of Britain and Ireland' iPhone app, published by Nature Guides in partnership with Bumblebee Conservation Trust and Habitat Aid. And If you capture any photos of bumblebees and you need help identifying them, the Bumblebee Conservation Trust are happy to help – you can submit them to the BeeWatch Survey and someone will get back to you with a confirmed identification.
- Build bee nesting boxes. These industrious creatures are a joy to watch in the garden. Creating a space where you can watch the bees build their nests is fascinating to adults and children alike. One easy method is to drill holes in a block of wood – a log or the end piece of a pallet box works very well. Drill a

series of holes of various diameter and leave above the ground in a protected location. Another easy option is to use reeds or bamboo. Cut 10cm long sections. It is important to leave one end of each tube blocked. Tie the sections together with string or wire. Again, place in an area which is protected from too much sun and wind. The tree bumblebee can nest in old bird boxes and so is easy to cater for.

- You don't need to have a garden to make a difference: rooftops and balconies can all play a part in providing a variety of bee-friendly plants. Native species are often most effective – they are adapted better to the climate of the area and have evolved in pace with native species of bees.

HOW TO PLANT YOUR GARDEN INTO A POLLINATOR'S PARADISE

In order for bees to meet their nutritional requirements, they need pollen, nectar and water. Nectar is a sugary energy source for the bees and pollen provides proteins and oils. The British Beekeeping Association recommends planting a wide variety of flowering plants that bloom between February and October.

Most garden centres can advise you on what bee-friendly plants will work in your area and the Royal Horticultural Society is an excellent source of information on what wild and garden plants are suitable.

Here is a starter list of what to plant:

Spring:
Rosemary, hawthorn, forget-me-not, crocuses, crab apple and cherry trees.

Summer:
Lavender, cosmos, hebe, Michaelmas daisy and yarrow.

Autumn:
Hydrangea, viburnum, common heather, red hot poker.

Lavender, rosemary, thyme, geraniums, borage and mint are hardy and will work well for your bees as well as in your kitchen.

15 *Minibeast hunt*

A Year Outside Challenge
23 May
Weather: Dry but overcast

We're in the park and I'm chatting to a friend, when the silence coming from the kids alerts me. We look around to see both my boys and my friend's girl lying, belly down, on the short grass. They are obviously watching something, and we approach slowly and quietly, not wanting to disturb their concentration, but also aware that they might well be watching something, a bug most likely, that could be easily scared away. A few seconds later, amidst screams and squeals of delight, they are all on their feet and following what I have now figured out is a grasshopper, keen to get away from the intense scrutiny. A.B.

As an early years teacher, the minibeast topic was always a favourite, enjoyed by both teachers and pupils alike. It offered a wealth of activities, both indoors and out, and there was something about 'life in the undergrowth', to borrow David Attenborough's phrase, that seemed to firmly grasp little ones' imagination. Minibeast hunts are a fantastic way to get children out and about, exploring the natural habitats of bugs and getting interested in their surroundings. Ideal spots include forests and other woodland, grassland, areas around ponds or streams, as well as, of course, a back garden or local park. I have successfully conducted minibeast hunts at a local green, as long as there is a thicket or a few trees and bushes.

Before you start, it is imperative to share some health and safety tips with your kids. Touching minibeasts with bare hands should not be encouraged, and do make them aware that many invertebrates can sting and bite: wasps and bees in particular, as well as ants, spiders and centipedes. Warn kids to handle all bugs with caution, as well as respect: it is very easy to damage frail wings and legs with rough handling. Finally, having the right equipment, like large spoons, a magnifying glass and a jar is helpful. If you are keen, you can get special 'minibeast pots' that incorporate a jar with holes and have some magnifying powers so that you can better observe your captive creatures.

Techniques vary, from net sweeping, to tree beating, in order to find creatures living in the canopy of trees. For my boys, log and rock turning turns out to be the easiest. After observing, always return the minibeasts to where you found them.

TAKING IT FURTHER

- There is a wealth of information on minibeast activities for school aged kids available online – from colouring sheets to creating your own minibeast acrostic poem and many others beside.
- Compile your very own minibeast reading list – visit the local library and find as many fiction and non-fiction books as you can find. Explore the world of minibeasts, before you go back outdoors to look for them. Knowing a little about the creepy-crawlies that you see can make the whole hunt a lot more fun, as well as more efficient, as you discover which plants and flowers they prefer.
- *The Very Hungry Caterpillar, The Grouchy Ladybug, The Mixed-up Chameleon and The Very Busy Spider*, all by much-loved children's author Eric Carle, offer a great starting point for kids, as well as inspiration for your own bug-inspired art. *Mad About Minibeasts,* by Giles Andreae and David Wojtowycz, will offer laughs and poetry inspiration.

- My favourite on the minibeast lifecycle, *Tadpole's Promise* by Jeanne Willis and Tony Ross, has a rather surprising ending!
- For older children non-fiction books and DVDs like the BBC's *Life in the Undergrowth* can create enthusiasm for invertebrates and their habits.

SUMMER

16 *Water play*

A Year Outside Challenge

14 June

Weather: Warm and humid

On days like this it appears my main purpose on this earth is making bubbles, blowing up balloons and spending inordinate amounts of time trying to inflate paddling pools. Of course I know I have a few more uses than my lung capacity, but at the moment exhaling into flaccid plastic tends to crowd them out. Today the sun succeeded in making things uncomfortable enough to persuade most people out into their cars in search of cool and solitude at the lido or beach, neither of which are likely to be found. Of course neither Joe nor Oliver have any intention of looking like the happy paddling children featured on the cover of the pool box and in a short while the pool is filled with every bowl and sieve and plastic cup we own. A very happy hour is spent dribbling, sieving and carrying water from the pool to every corner of our small garden. The kids are cool, happy and enjoy some creative play. D.B.

Water offers so many opportunities for hands-on, sensory exploration and imaginative play. It is one of these materials, just like blocks and sand, that provide truly open-ended play – there is no right or wrong way to use it.[1] And research shows that it is developmentally appropriate for all ages, regardless of a child's physical condition, language or gender.[2]

Sand and water play have been incorporated into early childhood curricula for years, but having access to natural watery settings combines the multiple benefits of instilling a love of the outdoors and observation of natural habitats with the relaxation benefits that nature in general, and water in particular, provide.

Water can have a rather therapeutic effect too: just think of the calming effect of a bath on infants, or the soothing effect on a pre-schooler of washing her face after a fall. Running water can soothe sensory overload, while aquariums have been found to

1 Crosser, S. (1994). Making the most of water play. *Young children, 49,* 28–38.
2 Bredekamp, S. (1987). *Developmentally appropriate practice in early childhood programs serving children from birth through age 8.* National Association for the Education of Young Children.

produce a marked physiological relaxation response: lowering of pulse rate, decrease in muscle tension and an increase in skin temperature have been observed.[1]

With a few basic safety tips, especially for little ones, kids of all ages can enjoy playing with water – and not just in summer either!

TAKING IT FURTHER

- Use a variety of tubs, spoons and ladles and different sized containers – young children love to pour and spill! Provide items that sink and some that will float and watch children turn into scientists who will make predictions as to what will stay afloat and what will head to the bottom.
- On very hot days, add coloured ice cubes to the water.
- Use water and brushes to 'paint' on concrete or tiles outside. Kids seem to happily spend ages water painting. The ephemeral nature of the task means that a few minutes later they can start on a new arty creation.
- On very hot days paddling pools and even buckets can be a fun addition to your outdoor time. A sprinkler can be a cheap way to entertain little ones in the back garden (if there is no hose-pipe ban).

1 DeSchriver, M. M., & Riddick, C. C. (1990). Effects of watching aquariums on elders' stress. *Anthrozoös*, *4*(1), 44–8.

17 Scavenger hunts

A Year Outside Challenge

19 June

Weather: Hot, dry

It is hot and dry and the grass has yellowed. The warm breeze does little to remove the haze. It is the kind of day you wait all year for, and we lay out our picnic blanket in the shade of a large leafy tree. Perfect. Just as we settle down with a feeling of utter contentment, a few sips of cool juice is all it takes for the kids to become bored and restless. Amazed at how quickly the mood can swing in little children, I know, glumly, that we can't all sit quietly and enjoy this perfect picnic spot. With some guilt, I come up with a game where I can 'hold the fort' while the children burn off some energy. A scavenger hunt! I try my best to make it sound as though it is the most exciting game ever. It works. A list is given and the children are off scampering and shouting. I reach for my hip flask (not really, but a man can dream). D.B.

Scavenger hunts are excellent at getting children to focus on a task and can even get small groups of children to work together. Teachers love variations of this game, either inside the class or out, as it teaches children social skills as well as problem solving ones. In its most basic form, you give a list of certain items to be found and either recorded or brought back, usually within a timeframe. The game lends itself perfectly to different age groups, occasions and locations. It is a game that you can prepare intricately far ahead of time or, if the situation demands, spontaneously. It essentially involves three simple steps:

- Set the limits to the area.
- Set out the items to be collected or recorded.
- Set a time limit.

GARDEN SCAVENGER HUNTS

These are like an Easter egg hunt but without the high emotional stakes of having to find chocolate before anyone else does. A garden is a safe controlled environment and lends itself well to small children. Different leaf sizes, shapes and colours, bird baths or bird feeders, ants, butterflies and spider webs are but a few of the many items you can add to your list. Using the same list for a friend's garden can add a fun twist.

OUTDOORS, PARKS AND OTHER AREAS

Much the same as with a garden scavenger hunt except over a wider area. As children are naturally inquisitive, exploring new locations will add to the fun enormously. Parks, campgrounds, beaches and family walks can all be transformed into frenetic hives of activity. A common sense approach needs to be taken in regards to safety. Simple rules like 'stay in sight of an adult' and 'don't turn over rocks or disturb wildlife' are important. Sorting children into groups with an adult team leader allows you to comb a wider area and you can add a few more exciting items to be found.

TAKING IT FURTHER

- Nature bingo: Create a bingo grid of 4 x 4 or 5 x 5 squares. You can get ideas online or use a prepared grid too. All the participants have to mark off whatever item they find. The first person or team to get a straight line – horizontal, vertical or diagonal – wins. This can be highly entertaining especially as other participants are bound to interpret the happy squeals of their competitors as meaning they are getting close to calling bingo! Nature bingo grids can be adapted easily to the location you are using and even the season.
- Collections runs: This is a scavenger hunt on the run! It can be adapted for any age, but works better with older children. Sticks, pebbles, leaves, litter can all be used. If you are doing an out and back course, leaving a token or some other form of 'proof' to be collected at the turn-around point is useful in ensuring everyone covers the distance. Up the stakes by putting time cut offs in place and penalties for items not found!
- Orienteering: Scavenger hunts are in many ways the junior equivalent of orienteering. In this version, simple maps of your local park can be made for the participants to follow and record or retrieve what they need to at each location. The complexity of the tasks and maps can be scaled appropriately for different age groups.

- Technology to the rescue: Many parents are concerned about excessive screen time on hand-held devices and look to excursions into nature for their children to switch off and engage with nature. But a good way to entice perhaps reluctant older children out is to let them do a scavenger hunt with their device, where instead of collecting something, they can take a photo of the list object, whether it is an insect, animal or plant. The opportunities are endless – using a smartphone for example, GPS coordinates might be logged for their findings. Another good example to explore one's local area is Geocaching. It is an activity where an item or container is hidden and to find it one needs to use a set of coordinates.

18 *Let's go fly a kite*

A Year Outside Challenge
28 June
Weather: Warm, overcast

A light breeze blows. Several tries are made to get the store-bought kite off the ground, but the light breeze seems unable to sustain it. Another try with the homemade one – made from reclaimed wood and a green rubbish bag. Then several moments of fun while the green kite soars up into the sky. The kids run, holding the string, laughing and enjoying themselves.

Squeals of delight echo and the six children up here with us take turns to hold the kite, running off into the distance in an effort to keep it going. Oliver watches closely, while Joe cannot wait for his turn. A.B.

Kite flying as a happy childhood activity is deeply ingrained in many of us. Children running with kites have appeared in everything from books to postage stamps the world over and in the film *Mary Poppins* the pastime is used to symbolise a happy, connected and wholesome family.

Whilst flying kites is always a thrilling activity for the young and old, making kites need not be seen as an obstacle to getting out there if you don't have a store-bought kite. You can usually knock up the simplest of kites in a few minutes and can spend days on more elaborate efforts. The scope for design and artwork is wide and you can easily find ways to involve your children no matter their age. From simple drawing, to careful measuring and cutting to a little trigonometry for those of the older and more begrudging age.

Many primary school teachers remark on the decline of fine motor skills in young children. Holding pencils and scissors are tasks that children can find awkward and tire from easily. It is a strong suspicion that it is due to screen time creep on younger and younger children. Interestingly a study has further found[1] that early

1 Piek, J. P., Dawson, L., Smith, L. M., & Gasson, N. (2008). The role of early fine and gross motor development on later motor and cognitive ability. *Human movement science*, *27*(5), 668–81.

motor performance can be used as a predictor of motor and cognitive performance of children once they reach school age. Kite building, as an activity under a watchful eye, incorporates most fine motor skills that children seem to need to develop and is fun to boot.

DIAMONDS IN THE SKY

One of the quickest to build and the most reliable to get airborne (an important criterion when your children have a stake in its success) is the diamond kite. In a pinch, two light bamboo sticks from the garden and a bin liner and you are most of the way there.

MATERIALS NEEDED

- Two sticks (5mm dowels or thin bamboo planting sticks of 1m in length)
- Plastic sheet or sturdy bin liner
- Tape (masking or duct tape)
- String for the tail
- Flying line (nylon or fishing line).

You don't have to follow the measurements I suggest, but use the ratios to build a smaller or larger kite if you need to.

MEASURING AND CUTTING THE SAIL

Fold your plastic sheet in half and lay it down on a flat surface. On the folded edge, measure a length of 1m and with a marker, put a dot on the 0cm, 75cm and 1m. At the 75cm mark, at 90 degrees, measure 50cm. This is where your cross spar will go. Join your dots and then carefully cut along the line of your folded plastic sheet. Unfold your plastic sheet and *voilà*, there's your diamond shape.

SETTING UP THE SPARS

Lay your centre spar first, tape the ends of your dowel to the sheet. Take care to trim your sticks if they are longer than the sheet. Lay your cross spar over perpendicularly and tape the dowel ends to the corners.

ADDING THE TAIL

Your tail is what adds stability, especially if it is quite breezy. Six times the length of your kite is a good starting length. You can always trim it shorter later. Cut your remaining plastic sheet or other materials of your choice into strips and tie them at even intervals along the tail string.

ATTACHING THE FLYING LINE

Prick a small hole where the dowels meet. Thread your flying line through the plastic and thread around the spars and tie firmly. When you fly your kite, the plastic sheet should face you, and the spars face away from you.

GO FLY A KITE

Never fly a kite near power lines, and be careful of others when flying a kite.

ROCK, SCISSORS . . . PAPER?

Using a roll of blank paper, you can get your children to draw or paint their own distinctive designs. Let the paper dry and then follow the directions above. The only extra step is to tape the edges all the way around your kite. This is to give some extra strength and prevents tearing. The paper kites aren't as durable, so pick your weather conditions for an outing carefully!

TAKING IT FURTHER

- For the dads that have difficulty giving up the kite string, NASA has designed a program just for you: the *Interactive Kite Modeler* (www.grc.nasa.gov/www/k-12/airplane/kite1.html).
- You can design your own kite and can change the size, shape and materials and see how the flight characteristics alter from each addition. And to boldly go, albeit virtually, see how your kite would fare on Mars!

19 Pond (and stream) dipping

A Year Outside Challenge

3 July

Weather: Wet but warm

We are by the local stream, exploring a new spot that we have not accessed before and Joe is wild with excitement. He is loving watching the stream carry the sticks he throws in and delights as they reach the short waterfall, disappear for a few seconds under the weight of the falling water, then reappear with a plop a bit further down. He watches one after the other and cannot get enough.

It is a little downstream, however, where the stream flattens into a wider, calmer section that he finds something he has not encountered before. In the rock pools formed in the flat rock he notices countless little black dots, speckled all over the river's edges. A.B.

HOW TO MAKE A POND DIPPING NET

Making your own pond dipping net is easy to do and a variety of odds and ends around the house can be cobbled together. A well-known DIY method makes use of a pair of tights, an old coat hanger and some tape. It is a great solution if you have a spontaneous trip to a pond, river or even rock pools on the coast.

Items needed: 1 pair of tights, 1 coat hanger, 1 roll of sturdy tape, 1 rod or stick, needle with large eye, fishing line or other string.

- Bend coat hanger into a diamond or circle shape
- Cut tights off at thigh level and tie leg pieces together
- Sew (or tape) waist onto the coat hanger
- Tape coat hanger to the stick
- Go pond dipping!

Hours of fun can be had exploring the shallow waters. Aside from their unlikely hope of catching a small fish in their net, the task offers an opportunity for children to catch and view many other important aspects of water ecosystems. Ponds and rivers support a diverse range of life and are excellent habitats for amphibians like toads and frogs as well as a host of invertebrates such as snails, water beetles and dragonflies that hunt above the water surface. One of my favourite aspects of pond dipping is the concept of food chains and how interrelated everything is.

In addition to your homemade net a few other items can really add to the experience:

- A camera – taking photos of an interesting catch can lead onto further exploration at home.
- Buckets and tubs. Margarine or ice-cream tubs work well as the white background makes your finds really stand out.
- Magnifying glass to get a closer look.
- Spoons can be useful as a safe and kind way to handle a catch if you need to move it from a bucket to a tub or back to its habitat.

20 Picnic time

A Year Outside Challenge
15 July
Weather: Clear and warm

Joe is bent over his bowl, concentrating on spooning lumps of porridge into his mouth, while Oliver munches on a piece of toast, jam all over his cheeks. I am savouring my coffee, enjoying the morning chill under several layers. The boys are still in their pyjamas as we enjoy our breakfast in the garden. It has become somewhat of a morning tradition since early spring, only stopped by rain or howling wind (though Duncan assures me we can have a tarp up for the former). It is a great start to the day, and although we only allow about twenty minutes for it, time seems to slow down when we are outdoors. Pinky, one of our dogs, lies expectantly under the picnic table. It's the perfect start to everyone's day. A.B.

Anyone with a back garden, or with access to a nearby green space can make a habit of some al fresco eating. Some of my fondest memories from my time living in south-west London include our afternoon/after-school picnics in Kew Green and Richmond Park. Offering a distinct end to the working day and signalling the beginning of leisure time, they happily punctuated my days as a teacher. Often joined by parents and pupils, each with their colourful blankets and small snacks, kids relished the space and time to enjoy the outdoors in an unstructured and unhurried way.

The thing is, a picnic does not have to be saved for a special occasion. Given the right preparation it can be a regular Saturday morning occurrence. A well-placed tarpaulin, or a more permanent structure, can provide shelter from light rain and make picnicking an option even on wet days.

Eating outside has been shown to improve our well-being, and there is even a study that supports the idea that eating in the open air can improve our mood and happiness.[1] More anecdotally children enjoy eating out, even if it is in the back garden, and I am a lot more relaxed when I know that the mess of breakfast will be cleared up by the birds afterwards. I'm also not sure if this is universal, but my two seem to eat a lot more when the novelty of eating outdoors is added to the mix.

Indeed, al fresco dining is a huge part of the Mediterranean culture and is elevated to an art in many settings. (Incidentally, the English usage of the phrase *al fresco* is quite far from the original Italian meaning, that means . . . time spent in jail. Instead, the Italians use the phrase *all'aperto* to mean out in the open.) For us, on the other hand, a more simplified version will have to do.

1 http://deliveringhappiness.com/happiness-increased-by-lunching-outside-the-office/ accessed 1 July 2016

Some useful tips for outdoor eating:

- Location, location, location – find a sheltered area that will be protected from the elements. Rain, wind or excessive sun can make the outdoor eating experience less fun.
- Choose a suitable picnic rug or blanket (with a waterproof bottom). Equally, a simple PVC coated tablecloth is easy to wipe, light to carry and cheap.
- If you are using your back garden regularly as a dining spot, consider investing in some outdoor furniture.
- Keep it simple. The simpler the food the better. Cold dishes, like sandwiches, fruit and vegetables and the odd treat is best. Avoid messy foods with sauces, or anything that requires separate serving utensils. Pack extra plastic boxes for any leftovers and rubbish.

Eating together, whether inside or out, seems to have a lot of benefits for children, and making some time to eat at least one meal a day together, although challenging for many families, can be very beneficial.

21 Camping

A Year Outside Challenge

5 August

Weather: Cloudy but dry, light breeze

Our first camping experience started off reasonably well, but things have swerved sharply for the worse. Bitterly, I mulled over an earlier conversation I'd had with a good friend about taking the family camping. Norman is a creature of comfort and had got into the procreation business earlier than I did and so I thought he'd have some good experience and advice in getting the family out camping and at one with nature. 'You are crazy for even suggesting that!' No advice there from someone who's been there and got burned.

I love camping and the urge to take my family with me is strong. Alexia agrees and the idea of a 'day camp' is a good one before we try anything more ambitious. We will set up the tent, spend the day, explore, have our afternoon nap and return home that evening, ruddy and wholesome. That is the plan, at least.

I am proud of the campsite I have found, a secluded leafy picnic area in the hills and I have managed to get the car close by. The tent is erected with minimal interference from the boys and a walk exploring the area has been fun with the boys trying drag as many sticks as they can to use for our pretend campfire.

Joe has spied ashes from an earlier fire and is adamant we should have one too. Miraculously he finds the idea of a pretend one to be just as agreeable. Lunch has to be eaten off sticks as we were camping after all. Fruit and sandwiches are duly skewered for the boys and roasted over our roaring pretend fire.

'Success! We have done it!' is all I proudly thought. No sooner have we zipped the tent closed and settled down for our nap when the sound of a small convoy of cars approaches. I pop my head out of the tent door only to see several families in several cars arriving and almost succeeding in completely encircling us. Tables, wine and platters of food are convivially unloaded with the car radios blaring.

We try in vain to coax the boys to sleep, but they know something far more interesting than sleep is outside and soon burst into tears, desperately trying to claw their way out. A half hour later, beaten, Alexia and I give up, and somewhat sweatily emerge from the tent to a look of palpable disapproval from a now quiet party. Joe and Oliver, overexcited and overtired, take turns wailing on the floor. Feeling ruddy faced and not for the hoped for reasons, we prematurely break camp and drive home after some awkward manoeuvring past the camp's new arrivals. Parts have gone well, but I got the location wrong and there is certainly more work to be done. I'm not going to prove Norman right. D.B.

Many parents are afraid of camping with children due to the change of routine, being stuck in a confined space and uncomfortable and sleepless nights. Yet the allure of unstructured kids' time outside, rosy childhood memories (even if fabricated) of sleeping under the stars, campfires, no screen time and what seems to be a golden opportunity for your children to be outdoors is great.

The love and appreciation of the outdoors is something you are able to pass on to your children, and one of the best ways to do that is through camping. You don't have to love camping to love the outdoors, though for many, camping is an integral part of experiencing nature. There are various levels of camping and various degrees in how closely you can get to feel you are in nature. For some it means a night under the stars in a comfortable campsite with many of the comforts of your home at hand. For others, on the wilder side of the spectrum, it is attractive to take little with you and to spend a night with only what you need, deep in the heart of the outdoors, yet all still under the same starry sky. All of my camping experiences I know have their roots in a tent set up in my parents' back garden when I was a child. Camping is indeed a wonderful way to experience nature and as a parent, it is a gradual journey of passing on confidence and skills to your children.

I decide to enlist the help of several experienced family campers and some new to the family camping scene to find what works for them, and what doesn't. John, father of two, is arguably the most experienced. Seasoned is the words he prefers, as he has seen it all over the years, from when his children were in the 'oven' to their current preteen years. Not only has he camped in far flung places like empty beaches in Mozambique and the salt pans of Botswana, but he regularly takes groups of teens into the wild as a school leader. Leo, father of one, an experienced ultra runner and quintessential mountain man, has not let the arrival of a baby put a stop to his camping habits. Cath, a pilates instructor and mother of two, enjoys regular camping trips in the English countryside and Rob, new to camping is just starting off. They are my fount of knowledge!

WHY ON EARTH WOULD YOU GO CAMPING?

It is not an uncommon question to be asked if you mention this out loud at a dinner among friends. Apart from my own reasons, reading and asking whoever I could, John's answer was perhaps the most considered. It wasn't only to do with what benefits nature gives to you, but what the experiences actually teaches children. After a decade of trips spanning the toddler years to near teens (and surely not all can have been good experiences), he believes that kids learn a great deal through camping. They learn how to be *resilient*, by doing campsite chores. *Creative*, as you make what you want of a campsite. How to *plan*, you take what you need – if you don't take it, you don't have it. Become aware of *low impact living* – commodities such as electrical supply and water can be scarce. Use what you need, save where you can. And finally, how to be *resourceful*, you have what you take with you, the rest you need to invent/find/make . . .

Camping is about: *Preparation, location* and *equipment*

PREPARE, PREPARE, PREPARE

Ideally a camping trip means getting away from it all, a break, a time to make do with less and enjoying oneself. The anticipation of going away has been shown to increase pre-trip happiness[1] – so get your children excited ahead of time by allowing them to be part of the planning stage of the trip. Ask them to organise what they would like to bring. Items such as teddy bears and other sleep companions have to share in the excitement of coming on the trip and often that familiar soft toy is all that's needed to get them nodding off after an exciting first day. This preparation stage, John notes, is important for kids as it helps them to feel that it is their trip as well, and not that they are just being 'dragged along'. His family spend time talking about what to expect, the things they might see or do, potential hazards, and what is expected behaviour. By the time they leave each member of the family has contributed with ideas and activities.

Although the anticipation of the trip can lead to a happier holiday, there is nothing worse than feeling that your camping trip is more work than organising supply depots from Everest Base Camp. Keeping an 'ongoing packing list' for your trips may seems like a lot of work, but it makes each subsequent trip easier. Adding things that you realised you needed and removing things that you didn't need helps make packing and organising future trips more efficient and, perhaps more importantly, it prevents the recriminations of 'I thought you packed it' over the missing roll of loo paper.

1 Nawijn, J., Marchand, M. A., Veenhoven, R., & Vingerhoets, A. J. (2010). Vacationers happier, but most not happier after a holiday. *Applied research in quality of life*, *5*(1), 35–47.

LOCATION

This is undeniably the most important step in camping with a family. Trips with the best equipment and idyllic locales have failed because the location has not been selected to fit the needs of the family. That remote five-night-away bucket list camping trip may need to wait.

Campsites and the amenities they offer vary enormously, from those with toilets, hot showers and communal washing up areas to others that are simply a cleared patch of field to set your tent up in. Do your research well! Campsites that offer some of the creature comforts of home are a good bet for the newbie camper and if you are camping with young children. Choosing a site that is not too far from a town may not feel like you are getting away enough, but it does allow for a useful degree of flexibility like the odd treat of an ice cream or, if the weather turns on you, somewhere dry to enjoy a meal. One of the aspects that Cath most enjoys is how quickly children make friends and how in no time her little ones are off in a small gang exploring and laughing. Rob, who had never been camping, found that camping with more experienced campers was an excellent learning experience: you can see what equipment they have and what works well. Consider it an informal mentorship and your children can learn the ropes from friends, who are – unfortunately – invariably cooler than mum or dad.

EQUIPMENT

I have a friend who bought a tent once purely on the basis that it was the brand and model used by some professional mountaineers, designed to withstand all the elements that could be thrown at it. Gloriously compact and light though it was, it failed to survive the rigours of camping with children. A larger, cheaper and heavier tent succeeded it. My point is, while it is wise to invest in good quality equipment, it has to be chosen by its uses. John explained that you have to know what makes you comfortable when camping. For him it is a comfortable mattress – good sleep is essential to counter grumpiness. Secondly, a good cool box or fridge. Leo and Elpida also make use of a dome shelter that is used as a general purpose area. It is tall enough to stand under, eat meals under and offers an alternative to the tent if one wishes to escape the rain or sun. Another excellent alternative is to string a large tarpaulin up between trees. Leo admits that even though they only free camp, they like to camp rather luxuriously. A gas cooker, portable chemical toilet and a battery powered fridge are indispensable. While this does seem contrary to the spirit of free camping, he argues it helps them manage their impact on the environment considerably. He never lights a fire, not only for fear of starting a woodland fire, but because gas is cleaner and uses no local wood for fuel. A chemical toilet likewise means that no human waste is left behind after their trip.

FOOD

Camping food needn't be akin to culinary deprivation. Yes, you won't have all the conveniences of your regular kitchen, but tasty food can also be simple. Hotdogs on a stick and roasted marshmallows, whilst not part of your normal nutritionally balanced diet, are a camping treat and are all part of the fun and the memories your children will be making. Not every meal needs to be prepared at camp either. Cath and her husband take an even simpler approach to food as they use the camp as a base for their holiday, cycling or driving to see the local attractions and sample some locally prepared food. In order to cut down on the food supplies they need to take, breakfast is eaten at camp and a packed lunch is prepared for the daily excursion. Evening meals are taken at a local restaurant. John's family cook once a day, generally in the evening. Leftovers and fresh foods are used for other meals.

SLEEPING AND SHOWERING

These are two areas that seem to put most people off camping, let alone going with children. Choose a campsite carefully and know what facilities are available regarding showers. If you are free camping a portable shower can wash off the day's excertions and will help you snuggle down more easily in your sleeping bag. Blow-up mattresses and pillows from home all help make a night's sleep under the stars more comfortable. Elpida immediately noticed that her toddler sleeps better and more soundly than at home, even though her family of three share a tent and a double mattress. She puts it down to full days spent engaged in a stimulating environment. Sleep for Rob and his family was of great concern. He found that having a few practice 'sleep outs' in the lounge before the trip helped enormously. The kids were still very excited on the first evening, but they were used to their sleeping bags, had their soft toys and were able to settle in. Routine is an essential part of a successful camping experience according to John. You are able to give kids less structured time but then make sure that the non-negotiable routine stays in place. They will come out with an understanding of the routines which you see as essential.

ENTERTAINMENT

Campsites are exciting and young children will be eager to explore and make friends. Board games, pond dipping nets and torches will provide hours of entertainment. Allow your children to bring some of their toys (within reason). Give them a finite amount of space, such as a plastic container or large re-sealable bag, so that they really consider what will be useful for the trip. Allowing children to entertain themselves is excellent for building creativity and is one of the best aspects of camping. Routines around entertainment are also a very good idea. Setting aside a quiet time each day, perhaps after lunch and for the entire family. A time for a nap, drawing, or playing a board game. Board games, books and a covered area to sit all allow for family time and are a great help when there is bad weather. Yet for those a little older and more obsessed with their phone or tablet, your idea of a weekend of getting back to basics in a Wi-Fi free zone might be a bit tough to accept. Compromise by downloading apps like *Geocaching* to hunt for caches in your area or *SkyView* to explore the night sky.

LEAVING ONLY FOOTPRINTS

Camping in campsites with amenities makes it a lot easier to manage the effect of your visit. For more exotic locations, Leo uses his equipment to lessen their impact on the environment. John and his family – due to where they go camping – can often go one better and try to have a positive impact on the environment. They try to remove any litter that they may find. Near one of the campsites they enjoy is a poorly resourced school, and they try to take writing and reading equipment with them and drop it off.

FIRST AID AND EMERGENCIES

All the families agreed that taking a well-stocked first aid kit was important. For anything more serious, ensuring a mobile is kept sufficiently charged and knowing the whereabouts of the nearest local hospital helps puts them at ease.

AUTUMN

22 Doing vs being (mindfulness)

A Year Outside Challenge

22 September (Autumn Equinox)

Weather: Light rain, light breeze, chilly

(Apparently) it is the first day of autumn. It is early morning, and light rain has fallen overnight, the smell of warm, wet earth permeating the whole garden. Joe is mesmerised by the leaves that have found themselves on the ground overnight, some still soft and only just turned yellow. I sit down with him and watch, patiently waiting for the newborn sun to send his rays our way. I then bundle him up into my embrace, both to warm him and to warm myself up. He curls up next to me, melts into my body and we spend maybe two minutes, maybe twenty, watching the leaves swayed by a soft breeze and taking in the morning smells and sounds of the garden in autumn. A.B.

In *Growing Up Happy* I wrote about the opportunities that being in nature gives us for simply 'being' as opposed to always 'doing', but I never thought that these would be so easily accessible to children of all ages. It started with my baby boy, who at around six months old used to love being outside and would simply stare at the leaves of the tree, caressed by the wind for an incredible amount of time, far more, that is to say, than I ever expected a child of his age to stay 'focused' for.

My eldest too, regularly enjoys simply being in nature, lying on the grass and watching clouds travel by, or listening to the birds. Such 'nature meditations' weave themselves in and out of our everyday experience seamlessly; we might be playing one minute, making mud pies and collecting pine cones, and the next Joe is captured by a sight, a smell or a sound and stops. Time stops. He sits and takes in all of nature, completely being.

As I am exploring meditation and mindfulness in my own life and have had a practice for a while, it resonates with me how children, when given the opportunity, can flit between the two states of being and doing naturally. Adults seem to find it harder, existing in a perpetual hamster wheel of doing. For this one I have to take a leaf out of my sons' book. Looking more deeply into nature meditations I find several practices that encourage me to do just what my boys seem to be doing. It appears that the open awareness of childhood is just what was needed to experience nature fully.

These moments never last long, and I never guide them, except perhaps by pointing out something worth seeing. But they enrich our days, amplify our time in nature and, I have no doubt, add to our well-being.

TAKING IT FURTHER

- For older children (seven year olds and upwards) a more formal practice can be established. One of the easiest ways to incorporate mindfulness meditation in natural surroundings (as well as indoors) is listening meditation. The beauty of using listening as a cue to focus attention is that sounds always happen in the present. Hence focusing on all the different layers of sound around us can bring us right into the moment, creating a true sense of inhabiting the present. Right here, right now!

23 *Wild food*

A Year Outside Challenge
27 September
Weather: Warm(ish) and overcast

Today the weather seemed to scream 'get outside!' The last few days before autumn is truly here and there is warmth in the air and a certain clarity that we know we will miss as winter approaches. We set forth determined on making the most of this very green and pleasant day. We have our baby carriers, food, supplies – we are ready. Alex and I trudge up the path each with a child strapped to our back. The hike is not going completely to plan. The reason for the outing, aside from the glorious weather, is to give Joe some space to run around. He has just recently realised that he can run and our house can no longer contain his energy. Like an itch one can't scratch, he can't bear to be still. So why – this idea so seemingly without flaw – was he stubbornly refusing to put his feet on the ground? A short while into the hike we are passed cheerfully by a young couple unadorned by children. Joe waves them on with a cheerful 'good day' and smiling beneficently from his perch with no sign of wanting to get down. A few bends in the trail later we bump into the young hikers again. They have stopped and are picking blackberries. Joe is instantly interested in what they are doing and so starts protesting that he wants, immediately, to get down. Having grown accustomed to the stage of parenting where nothing should be put in the mouth I am a little uncomfortable with opening up an exception just yet. But they are blackberries and the two hikers are grabbing handfuls of them. I acquiesce, mostly because neither of them has collapsed or is frothing at the mouth. Joe picks his own, plops one in his mouth and almost instantly smiles, drooling a lovely deep purple onto his T-shirt. For the rest of the hike he skips ahead, fascinated, from shrub to shrub like a bumblebee. D.B.

Foraging for food with our children wasn't something I had expected to do, but Joe's interest was piqued and I knew that we had to put some rules in place. That and our years in Greece had been filled with tasty and locally sourced natural foods. In autumn and spring, a common sight along the untended roadsides, empty fields and up in the hills is elderly men and women armed with plastic bags and kitchen knives. They are looking for a selection of wild greens that are used for homemade pies and salads.

REASONS TO FORAGE

- It breaks down the barrier there is now between children and the environment.
- It strengthens the bond between children and their environment.
- The education is empowering.
- Children sync up and experience the seasons in an entirely different way.
- Wild edibles are nutritious, fun to forage for and provide an interesting change to eating routines.

WHERE TO START

- Some of the best wild edibles to begin with are the sweet obvious ones, blackberries and mulberries, with the added benefit that they don't have any poisonous lookalikes.
- Have a *don't-put-it-in-your-mouth-until-you-check-with-me-first* policy for the little ones.
- Learn what some of the dangerous plants are in your area. This will give you a bit of confidence in knowing what to stay away from.
- Remove only the part of the plant you will use.

- Don't over harvest.
- Sign up to a foraging course!
- If you decide to stray from the obvious wild edibles you need to be properly educated or have a mentor. That's not to put you off foraging, it's a wonderful pursuit that puts you in touch with nature and takes time and experience, but staying safe while doing it is paramount.

Foraging for food in the wild is something that seems to satisfy a deep human need, and taps well into our evolutionary past. A study on non-human primates, which might provide clues on our evolutionary past, links early learning with just these foraging behaviours. It seems that some of the most important information these apes pass on to their young is complex foraging methods, about what, where and how to eat.[1]

For us as a family foraging for wild food does not develop into a frequent activity. It does, however, provide some sort of extra incentive for our little ones on hikes, as they delight in spotting edible plants, fruits and the occasional mushroom (which we never quite dare to eat).

1 Rapaport, L.G. and Brown, G.R. (2008). 'Social influences on foraging behavior in young nonhuman primates: learning what, where and how to eat'. *Evolutionary anthropology: issues, news and reviews*, 17 (4), 189–201.

24 *Leaf art*

A Year Outside Challenge
1 October
Weather: Light breeze, chilly but dry

Our walk at the local park has been hijacked by Joe's insistence on collecting leaves for his pictures. He's holding a plastic bag, quickly filling with different types of leaves, some dry and some not so much. He does not stop at this, though: small sticks, bits of weeds and flowers also end up in the bag, to be sorted later. Oliver, ever keen to join in, starts picking up leaves and soon my rucksack is starting to fill too. It seems to be keeping both boys interested in exploring, though, and the walk becomes more of a treasure hunt: the excitement at finding a different colour or an odd shape is certainly great!

I'm visiting Melanie, mum of eight-year-old Leah, on a grey autumn day to chat about art projects. Melanie is an artist by trade and inclination, and everywhere I look there are small and large works of art: from her handmade earrings to pictures hanging on her staircase. My attention is drawn, however, to some carefully framed pictures in her kitchen – when I look closely I see that the animals in the frame are a combination of leaves and flowers, dried and pressed, then combined to create a lion, a hedgehog, a peacock. I am impressed, but feel this is unattainable for me and my kids.

'Leah and I have been experimenting with nature art for several years – this is the result of that,' she tells me when I ask her. 'You can't expect to produce this the first time you sit down to make a picture.'

She opens an album and shows me some more: this time whole landscapes, complete with bright suns, roaring seas and houses. Some of the leaves are as they were on the tree, some have been altered to fit the picture. The occasional line of colour has been added to help make sense of each sketch, while some other compositions are simply left as . . . nature intended them.

There are a couple of secrets, Melanie tells me and she promises to take me with her on a collecting walk. In fact, we are not going far – it is autumn and there are leaves everywhere, once you start looking for them. We walk to school to pick Leah up and then on the way back we take a detour through a very small local park. We each carry a bag and are on the look-out for any special shapes or different shades. Pine needles, wide plane tree leaves, as well as thin willow leaves all make it into the bag.

'The secret is to collect widely – don't think about your picture yet, but collect what takes your fancy. And don't just limit yourself to one or two of each kind – take a few more, because even the smallest random variation in shade or shape can be the beginning of something.'

I listen, and like a good student, collect a big bag full of golden, yellow, brown and some green leaves.

'Another thing that is worth doing is coming out again in a few weeks' time, before you start composing.' She explains why to me, and I'm eager to go out in a couple of weeks. 'Different trees will lose their leaves at slightly different times – by waiting a while you have more of a chance to create a greater variety in your collection.'

Two weeks later I go out again, this time on my own and in a different piece of woodland, near a stream. I collect another bagful and add them to the layers of drying leaves in my garage.

It is almost Christmas when my little ones and I actually find time to sit down and start on our very own leaf pictures. Joe, at three and a half, loves the creative process and is able to 'see' animals, and other objects a lot more readily than I can! He combines different colours and shades expertly and creates a whole zoo worth of animals, with gusto. Even Oliver, at two years of age, enjoys putting together different shapes, though he prefers making cars and tractors . . .

Although our pictures are nowhere as impressive as the ones Melanie and Leah have made, I take comfort in Melanie's word and chalk it up as a success. The collecting walks, as well as the indoor activity were a way for my boys to go out to nature, and bring nature into our homes. On top of that, I am going to use some of the pictures the boys lovingly made as unique, homemade Christmas cards for our loved ones. A win-win situation, for sure!

TAKING IT FURTHER

- It seems that the more diverse your collection sites, the more likely you are to have the 'right' shape and shade for your picture. Enjoy several walks outdoors, before you sit down to work on your leaf art.
- If you find particularly beautiful leaves that you might want to keep for ever, you can laminate them. You can then hang them from a branch (alternatively you can use an old-fashioned wire hanger, bent into shape) to make a beautiful baby mobile, or home decoration.

25 *Natural collections*

A Year Outside Challenge
5 October
Weather: Overcast and drizzly

Joe is adamant he has to carry the sticks back to the car. He has three in one hand, and a couple more sticking out of his waistband. He has given me a big one to carry and is now considering placing some underneath his brother's seat on the buggy.

I indulge him and secretly quite enjoy the excitement a mere stick is providing. I let him put them in the boot of the car at the end of our walk, and help him carry them into the garden, where he spends the rest of the day sorting them. His brother curiously looks on, but is forbidden from touching them. Instead I help Oliver start his own collection of little cypress cones, which are sprinkled all over our back yard.

That night I get out my own pebble collection. It spans about ten years of travel – from New Zealand to South Africa – and includes a pebble from a Cornish beach and one from Vancouver Island, a stone from Mount Olympus and even a little jar of black sand from the volcanic island of Santorini. On each specimen there is a place name and a date. I look fondly at a pebble my husband (then boyfriend of only a few months) offered me after a run up the local mountain.

I'm sure there is a special place reserved in hell for adults who collect pebbles, but I put away my collection with fond memories of each and every place I have visited. A.B.

There is a certain beauty in natural collections, whether they are of sticks (yes, my son is three and he loves to collect sticks) or of the most peculiar insects, if you are an entomologist. I remember visiting the Natural History Museum as a young child and being amazed at the collections of colourful butterflies and gigantic beetles, all carefully pinned in endless rows. I remember wondering just how they were captured, and hoping that the entomologist in charge had waited until the butterflies had died of natural causes before adding them to his collection. I'm afraid I might have been wrong . . .

It seems that collecting bits of nature, to bring into our houses, is universal and can start at a rather young age. From as young as two, children will collect simple natural objects, like sticks, leaves or flowers. When encouraged they will compare and contrast them, order them by size, group them by colour or simply cherish them and add to them.

In an article on how infants and toddlers meet the natural world, infant education specialist Jolie McHenry suggests offering infants natural objects, like leaves or pine cones, to investigate.[1] She talks about bringing these into the childcare setting, but also taking children out on nature walks.

At home, with a much better ratio of child to carer, nature collection walks are easier to undertake. In fact, a parent can simply put the idea out there and then watch the children as they

1 McHenry, J. D. & Buerk, K. J. (2008). Infants and toddlers meet the natural world. *Young children*, *63*(1), 40.

hunt down different leaves, flowers or colourful stones. A trip to the beach, up a mountain or even to the local park will never be the same again!

Natural item collection can give purpose to even the shortest stroll. Duncan often takes the boys out for a short, twenty-minute walk round the block, to look for wildflowers. The idea of looking for something makes the walk more pleasurable for the boys, and the additional offering of their small, wildflower bouquet for mummy gives them the extra incentive they need.

Equally, walks on the beach become more fun when looking for glass pebbles, coloured stones, or driftwood. Care needs to be taken, though! Collecting needs to be done with respect and thoughtfulness towards the environment. Children need to be taught the effect our collecting can have on local organisms. For this reason, collecting shells should be avoided.

A study of coastal environments in Spain[1] warns that shell-collecting from the shoreline can have an adverse effect on local organisms. Availability of habitat (many small creatures live in abandoned shells), as well as in calcium carbonate recycling, declines in diversity and abundance of organisms, are all dependent on shell availability. Removing them from the beach is

1 Kowalewski, M., Domènech, R., & Martinell, J. (2014). Vanishing clams on an Iberian beach: local consequences and global implications of accelerating loss of shells to tourism. *PloS one*, *9*(1), e83615.

an act of damage and we should educate ourselves and our children against it.

TAKING IT FURTHER

- Use your collections to great effect. Decorate your home with fresh wildflowers, press leaves and flowers (in a flower press, or between the pages of a heavy book) or use pebbles and rocks as decorative elements in your house.

26 *Rainy day fun*

A Year Outside Challenge
10 October
Weather: Wet, chilly

The rain comes down, at first slowly, then relentlessly. I look from behind the curtain, trying to work out if better weather is round the corner, or if I should take the plunge and dress the boys up for our afternoon walk in waterproofs. They can hardly contain their excitement at donning their wellies – Joe especially keeps reminding me about all the snails we saw last time. And so we venture out, on a great snail chase . . . A.B.

I am surprised to learn that snails (and slugs, it turns out) are mainly nocturnal creatures. However, soon after the rain stops on this autumn day, they seem to start coming out in droves. I am amazed at how good the boys are at spotting snails – possibly because they are a lot closer to the action than I am.

Similar to the minibeast hunt, but better on a wet day, snail hunts can be great fun for toddlers and young children. Hunting for snails does not require huge amounts of space, as even the smallest garden will have its fair share. Local parks can also offer a good spot to look for the shy invertebrates.

Joe quickly finds a few, and places them on a flat rock on the table. They seem happy to go about their business, under the watchful eye of the two boys. They later get placed back in the garden bed and go back to looking for Duncan's juicy lettuce and spinach leaves.

TAKING IT FURTHER

- Some excellent snail picture books include *Snail Trail*, by Ruth Brown and *Are you a Snail?* (Up the Garden Path), by Judy Allen and Tudor Humphries.
- For a heart-warming tale of a (sea) snail and its friend, the whale, which will provide inspiration when looking for silvery snail trails in the garden read *The Snail and the Whale by Julia Donaldson and Axel Scheffler.*

PUDDLE FUN

There is nothing more fun for kids, it seems, than jumping into puddles. Getting wet and muddy, splashing others and having unrestrained fun is always easier if you have the right gear. Find the deepest, muddiest puddle and see who can make the biggest splash, or follow rain water as it travels down a slope in a newlymade stream. (If you have come in a car make sure you have a spare set of clothes to drive back in and a few bags to put the wet kit into.)

TAKING IT FURTHER

- Make a game out of jumping in muddy puddles by starting a competition for kids to see if they can jump over and clear a puddle. If they do, they get a point. If they don't? Well, that's where all the fun is!

27 *Mud pies, stone soup and other delicacies*

A Year Outside Challenge
4 November
Weather: Wet

What to do on the muddiest, wettest day of the year? It has been raining overnight, and it's still pouring down heavily. I'm more than happy to sit under the porch, dry (but not warm), and watch the boys, all dressed in their waterproofs, enjoy the garden. Our small back garden has gained several shallow puddles, and is full of mud round the edges. Both boys are delighted to be out. Oliver uses his spade to dig out big dollops of the oozy stuff, then puts it onto his plate. Bit by bit he piles it on, with as much care as he can muster. He then looks around for decorations – leaves, little stones and twigs go on and the cake is ready to serve! A.B.

Playing in the mud might not be every mum's favourite, especially its aftermath, but the benefits for children are numerous. As a material, mud is extremely versatile and, on rainy days, abundant. It offers the kind of open-ended play that sparks creativity! Similar to clay or plasticine, mud has the added benefit of being free (!) and readily available in most outdoor settings. Moreover, naturally occurring bacteria found in mud and soil, like the *Mycobacterium vaccae*,[1] have been linked with the mood-boosting chemical serotonin.

When left to their own devices in the presence of muddy abundance, my little ones usually embark on a bake-athon, with mud pies and cookies being the favourite 'outcomes'. Depending on the kind of mud you have available, as well as the amounts of water you have at hand, other possibilities emerge, including mud soup, smoothies, etc.

Duncan builds a mud kitchen (p. 147) and I take it upon myself to equip it. I don't want to spend too much on it, so I ask friends and family for donations of old pots and pans and other kitchen utensils they no longer use. A baking tin, an old frying pan, ladles

1 'Getting Dirty May Lift Your Mood' http://www.bristol.ac.uk/news/2007/5384.html accessed 12 May 2015

and spoons and some old plastic plates and cups are gratefully received, both by me and the budding chefs. I also buy them some cheap cupcake cases, and they enjoy making and decorating mud cupcakes for everyone.

I am amazed at how engaged the boys are while playing in their kitchen. This type of play incorporates all sorts of elements: social interaction and role play, creativity, an open-ended medium and, of course, it is all outdoors! Although in the past I would have categorised mud play as solitary, I am impressed at just how much social interaction there is. They are negotiating the use of tools and space expertly and combine skills to create various culinary delights. They even role play, as Joe pretends to be daddy (!) and asks his little brother to help him out with the cooking.

On another occasion, in the company of two older friends, aged six and eight, a whole restaurant materialises, with the little ones working in the kitchen, while the two older girls come and take our orders, and serve us a seemingly never-ending, several-course meal. Deliveries are made, dishes are sampled and imaginary money changes hands, while we enjoy being out in the garden.

TAKING IT FURTHER

- **Sculpture** If you have the right type of soil (the silkier, or more clay-like it is, the better) then you can use it to make free-standing sculptures, which you can even dry and keep. The more sandy your soil is, the harder it will be to keep any of your sculptures, but that should not put you off creating creatures, structures or anything else. Your imagination is the only limit.

- **Drawing and painting** Mud can be used either as paint on a natural or other surface, or as the surface itself. If you want to use mud as paint make sure it is 'wet' enough. You can use it on paper, canvas or simply on tiles. It can be left to dry, or simply washed off afterwards. If you want to use it as the canvas itself, then you need some sort of plate or baking tray. Lay out a thin layer of mud and use a stick, a fork or other implement to 'draw'.
- **Mosaics** Pine cones, sticks, flowers, leaves, stones and wood shavings can all be collected beforehand to create beautiful mosaics, with mud as the base.

MAKING A MUD KITCHEN

Pottering about in a mud kitchen is another activity that will keep your children engaged for hours on end. Mud kitchens are a lot of fun to set up and you can use numerous odds and ends to create something that will spark your children's imagination. What we have found works best is to have something robust. It doesn't need to be beautifully painted. After its first use it'll probably never look the same again!

A few pallets are an excellent starting point. A box that opens and closes is also a favourite, as it can turn into an oven or just a cupboard. Using a wall or boundary fence as part of your design gives you more options to continue adding to the kitchen or to hang pots and pans on. Being close to a water source isn't imperative as children love ferrying water about and is absolutely part of the fun. You will, however, want to hose down the surfaces every now and then. Leaves and twigs are essential ingredients and if you are protective over some of your shrubs, it's best to plant a few sacrificial 'kitchen plants' nearby. Another fun activity is to 'forage' for leaves and twigs that have fallen to the ground when you are out for a walk, as these can then be used for cooking.

A few ideas for things to include in your design:

- A surface (hob) to cook on.
- Something that opens and closes to store or bake things in.
- An old or a make-believe tap.
- Old pots, pans, baking trays for delicious concoctions to be made in.

28 The forgotten art of tree climbing

A Year Outside Challenge
12 November
Weather: Cold and crisp

I have joined my friend Miranda and her two girls at their local park. It is the perfect autumn day, cold but sunny and the wind has thankfully died down to a breeze. Still, the cold cuts through my thick winter coat, my fleece and two layers of undershirt. The children on the other hand seem fine. Joe has joined Miranda's two girls, seven and five, at trying to climb onto a tree that has seen better days. The pine tree's roots are hanging onto the soil for dear life, literally, while its branches are brushing the ground. Its trunk is at a 30-degree angle to the ground, making it perfect for a first attempt at tree climbing. A.B.

The history of tree climbing goes back into the mists of time, merging our species history with that of our evolutionary ancestors. It seems that hunter-gatherers the world over have used tree climbing as a way to access food.[1] One of the most valuable foods accessed this way seems to be honey, with fruits, nuts and seeds also being reasons why humans have defied gravity and taken to the branches. A non-food reason to take to the canopy is to avoid potentially dangerous animals, such as elephants and lions.[2]

A study that compared climbing live trees to climbing a concrete tower in terms of physiological and psychological benefits, found that climbers' bodies were physically more relaxed after climbing a live tree, while psychological benefits of the tree versus the tower

1 Kraft, T. S., Venkataraman, V. V., & Dominy, N. J. (2014). A natural history of human tree climbing. *Journal of human evolution*, *71*, 105–18.
2 Coss, R. G., & Moore, M. (2002). Precocious knowledge of trees as antipredator refuge in preschool children: An examination of aesthetics, attributive judgments, and relic sexual dinichism. *Ecological Psychology*, *14*(4), 181–22.

included reduced tension, confusion and fatigue and increased vitality.[1] Further research suggests that tree climbing can have therapeutic benefits for individuals, but also could be socially beneficial, affecting participants in ways that make them more environmentally conscious.[2]

A million miles away from the nearest soft play, tree climbing offers children multiple benefits. One of them is the ability to judge and manage risk. As discussed at the beginning of the book, relying on outside risk managers (parents, teachers, older siblings, rules) to help you manage danger can result in greater harm when unconstrained. Instead, leaving kids to develop their own sense of danger, to test their own limits and adjust their expectations according to their own abilities can lead to children taking greater care, and ultimately avoiding overstepping their own marks.

For a good percentage of parents, we are simply too scared to let our kids explore without setting some sort of limits. It's a steep learning curve for all of us, the children learning the limits, and us parents learning to let go, a little bit at a time. I chat to Jane, a much more experienced mum of three. We have come to a nearby

1 Gathright, J., Yamada, Y., & Morita, M. (2006). Comparison of the physiological and psychological benefits of tree and tower climbing. *Urban forestry & urban greening*, *5*(3), 141–9.
2 Gathright, J., Yamada, Y., & Morita, M. (2008). Tree-assisted therapy: therapeutic and societal benefits from purpose-specific technical recreational tree-climbing programs. *Arboriculture and urban forestry*, *34*(4), 222.

playground, and yet the kids, instead of playing on the swings or climbing on the monkey bars, insist on climbing on a nearby tree. And who can blame them – the tree is just perfect! She is happy to let them explore their limits, safe in the knowledge that they have the experience to judge what is dangerous and what is not. And sure enough, all of her kids seem to set their own limits very sensibly – one manages to climb very high up the tree, while another prefers to stay much lower, on the thicker and more stable branches. I watch with delight, as do Joe and Oliver, from the safety of their own perches nearby.

TAKING IT FURTHER

- The older the child, the more likely they are to want to tackle bigger trees. Remind them of a few simple rules. It is wise to check for rotten or old branches before they put their weight on them – often inspecting the trunk and around the base of a tree will give you valuable information on the state of its health and strength. Fungi growing out of it, large holes or cracks, or a considerable number of dead branches on the ground should warn you to stay off. Removing your shoes will most likely offer you better grip, while you should make sure your clothing is not so loose that it catches on nearby branches. Finally, be aware of wild bee and wasp nests, and leave them undisturbed!

29 Running

A Year Outside Challenge

3 December

Weather: Light rain, light breeze, chilly

When our youngest started to lurch about on two legs, seemingly drawn to every sharp and pointy item of furniture in the house, I was rather surprised. Firstly, it seemed as though it happened overnight. Secondly, after perfecting the art of crawling and climbing up and down stairs safely and alarmingly quickly, the urge to try walking, awkwardly on two legs seemed largely counterintuitive on his part. But there was no stopping him, no matter the number of falls he suffered. Despite the difficulty, one look at his wide-eyed expression and fixed grin, his exhilaration was evident: he had found a new and exciting way to see the world.

Now, a few months later our eldest son is at the next stage and has similarly found excitement in running, or should I rather call it moving quickly. He runs for short stretches alongside the buggy, swinging his right elbow more energetically than his left as he maintains earnestly that this makes him fast. His steps are quick and light and unthinkingly natural. When we go for a walk in a park he can't help himself: he runs on ahead of us, zigzagging from one item of interest to the next, immersed completely in his surroundings. It looks like the definition of fun. D.B.

Hardly a week goes by without a headline crowing about the sad state of our youth. Obesity rates are soaring and exercise levels are plummeting. Many of the articles are so shrill and alarming that you will think twice before picking up a discarded newspaper on the tube or bus ever again. Worryingly, a 2016 Public Health England paper[1] showed that one in five Reception age children are either obese or overweight. By the time the children get to Year 6, one out of three children will be. Whilst exercise isn't always the whole solution, the benefits of exercise are clear and many, from enhanced cardiovascular metabolic health to improved confidence and peer acceptance. Working out whether running is a suitable activity for children isn't always easy. The myth that running ruins your knees continues to persist stubbornly. Happily, a recent study[2] found that runners were significantly less likely to develop arthritis than walkers. That's not to say you won't get injured with running: you can if you don't heed the warning signs of niggles and over training – just as one would with other sports.

Paediatricians are divided on how much running is too much. Many feel that children are proven to be more susceptible to repetitive stress injuries and running is one form of exercise that can have long-term consequences. However, evidence for the harmful

1 Statistics on Obesity, Physical Activity and Diet. (28 April 2016). Retrieved 20 July 2016 from http://www.hscic.gov.uk/catalogue/PUB20562/obes-phys-acti-diet-eng-2016-rep.pdf accessed 2 August 2016
2 Williams, P. T. (2013). Effects of running and walking on osteoarthritis and hip replacement risk. *Medicine and science in sports and exercise*, *45*(7), 1292.

long-term effect of running on children isn't there. A paper from the American Academy of Paediatrics[1] stated that provided a young athlete is asymptomatic and enjoys running, there is no reason to disallow them from participation. So, in regards to letting your child run, a common sense approach is best.

THE SCIENCE BEHIND LETTING YOUR CHILD RUN A LITTLE WILD

Before and during the teenage years, bone development increases significantly. When you are young, your body makes new bone faster than it breaks down old bone and your bone mass increases. Post adolescence, in your early twenties, you will have reached your bone mass peak. New bone creation will, from then on, be slower than old bone loss. How much bone you have generated in these early years is a strong predictor of how likely you are to develop osteoporosis. You can increase your muscle strength and cardiovascular fitness but there is little you can do for your bones by that stage. And if the development of bone mass isn't persuasive enough, perhaps the statistic that if your child is active and healthy, they could earn up to 30 per cent more than their contemporaries later in life will be! An intriguing Finnish study[2] that began in the 1980s assessed the physical activity levels

1 Brenner, J. S. (2007). Overuse injuries, overtraining, and burnout in child and adolescent athletes. *Pediatrics, 119*(6), 1242–5.
2 Kari, J. T., Tammelin, T. H., Viinikainen, J., Hutri-Kähönen, N., Raitakari, O. T., & Pehkonen, J. (2016). Childhood Physical Activity and Adulthood Earnings. *Medicine and science in sports and exercise, 48(7), 1340–1346.*

of 3,000 children when they were nine, twelve and fifteen years old. By 2010, after the data was linked to tax records, amongst the men, even when accounting for family and social status, those who were more physically active earned 30 per cent more than contemporaries (the bad news is that this applied only to boys). Another benefit is that increased cardiovascular fitness in teenagers was linked with better cognitive scores according to a Swedish study.[1]

Furthermore, setting goals with your children and working to succeed in accomplishing them not only is an important life skill, but also a wonderful motivator that builds confidence and self-esteem. But be wary of setting goals too early that are too big or will take too long to achieve. Goals that are too far in the distance, like being able to run a 5k, are too intangible. More appropriate fun and short term goals have greater meaning.

WHEN AND HOW TO START GETTING THEM TO RUN WILD, HEALTHILY

Children aged two to six

This is the time children develop their gross motor skills. The stimulation they receive from movement and sensory experiences are all key parts of early brain development, and learning to move

1 Åberg, M. A., Pedersen, N. L., Torén, K., Svartengren, M., Bäckstrand, B., Johnsson, T., . . . & Kuhn, H. G. (2009). Cardiovascular fitness is associated with cognition in young adulthood. *Proceedings of the National Academy of Sciences, 106*(49), 20906–11.

about means that their muscles and nerves are all functioning in sync. Coordination, balance and confidence are all learnt as they stagger and wheel about. Running is clearly fun for toddlers and you can't help but notice the squeals and smiles as they learn to move at speed. From once they can start walking to when they have developed an adult style of walk and run, which is usually around the age of six or seven, running is about you providing opportunities for your children to be active and to have fun – preferably outside. There are many ways to do this: by going to a park and getting them to chase a ball for example, or challenging them to run to and climb over a nearby log. Fly a kite, chase soap bubbles, catch a ball, play hide-and-seek – all ways to get children to move (and all to be followed by a big hug!). Running, jumping, speeding up, slowing down, getting up all serve to build muscles and bones.

Children aged seven to eight

At this age, running should be free from pressure and child led. Children that love and enjoy running can take part in fun runs. Often races will have a kiddies' run that they can take part in. Parkrun events are another wonderful alternative – they take place in parklands, are timed and free. They have 2k and 5k races. Clubs with organised children's running programmes provide another good opportunity for your child to run with others. The focus at this age should be on all-round fitness and coordination without an overt specialisation on running. Taking part in a variety of sports is the best way to go.

Teens

By the time most boys and girls have become adolescents, they will have developed enough to begin more run-focused training. Low mileage with short bouts of intensity can be undertaken safely. A recent University of Bristol[1] study found that running and jumping in adolescents helps develop bone mass and sturdier hip bones. Even if running starts to become a focus, it is important that they cross train. The urge to specialise at this age is great especially if promise is shown in a youngster.

HOW TO START RUNNING WILD ON THE TRAILS

Start them early

Children are naturally inquisitive and finding new places to explore will encourage them to run. As children get older, their lives will 'fill' rather quickly with other interests and school pressures. They might not have the inclination to try something new. If your child loves football or tennis, trail running is an excellent cross training activity.

Short and sweet

Start off with short distances of less than 5k. The distance depends on the age and activity levels of your child – take an approach of quality over quantity. Focus on time rather than on distance when you are on the trails and especially when you are with little ones.

1 Tobias, J. H., Steer, C. D., Mattocks, C. G., Riddoch, C., & Ness, A. R. (2007). Habitual levels of physical activity influence bone mass in 11-year-old children from the United Kingdom: findings from a large population-based cohort. *Journal of bone and mineral research*, *22*(1), 101–109.

Avoid going a bridge too far

Knowing when to stop your run, even if it is going well, is very important. Finishing a run miserable and tired won't help in them wanting to run the next time. If you have done enough and they want more, they'll be keen for the next outing.

Run and walk

First and foremost the run needs to be treated as an outing into nature, a chance to explore. Walk up a hill, look at the view, smell the flowers and let them hurtle downhill if they want.

They're in charge

To a point. Don't let them feel like they are being dragged around by you. Give them the opportunity to pick the pace and lead the run.

Be prepared

Going fast and light doesn't apply when running with kids on the trail. Make sure you have a small snack or drink of water if they need. A small plaster for a grazed knee can make the difference between finishing and you carrying your child back because they don't want to go on any more.

It's all about the child

A run on the trails with your child shouldn't be seen as a training session for you unless you have a strong runner on your hands. It is important that the pace and distance and time is focused on the child's needs. If you are also training, try to get your run in beforehand or afterwards.

TAKING IT FURTHER – MAKING RUNNING FUN AGAIN

- A change of scenery. A park, the track, a dirt road, a night run all keep it different and interesting.
- Have a laugh. Kids love fun and games. If you have a group Simon Says, Duck Duck Goose, Grab a Tag, Traffic Lights all work well for having a good time from a warm up to sweaty running fun.
- Make it personal. Children are very quick to compare and rank themselves against their peers. Adults are the same, but with young children this ranking often can lead to a fixed negative mindset as to their ability that will be difficult to change. Get children to run against their personal best times. It is better for them to see the value and experience a sense of improvement when they better themselves rather than focusing on the result, especially if they finish consistently near the back of the pack.
- Take a break. Sometimes you should just do something else altogether. Instead of training, have a game of football or play tag. The kids are still active and, importantly, are bonding and having fun.
- Volunteer to marshal a race and let them get inspired from the other side. Cheer on and support runners at a local race. It is an important lesson to help others, even if it's a small gesture of vocal encouragement and a cup of water.

- Fun photos. Take photos of runs in special places. A friend of ours routinely takes photos of her children running in well-known locations when on holiday. Her favourite photo is of her daughter jogging around the piazza in front of St Peters in Rome. Even though these 'runs' are short and light-hearted, they have become a family highlight whenever they go on holiday. Display them and remember all the fun times!
- Grab a head torch and head out into the night. Run somewhere that you know well and is safe. Running along in your own little light beam is a bit like running with blinkers. Your world is condensed into a few metres. Time and distance disappear and you will have loads of fun.
- Scavenger Run (page 106). What child doesn't love a scavenger hunt? Think of an Easter egg hunt with running. Go to a local park or field, make a map and let them go wild.
- Collection run. Set a task where a few items need to be collected within a certain time. Three different tree leaves, an acorn, a feather, a pebble. Make up a list of things to collect that are reasonable given the season and location and have fun watching them scamper around looking for things. They can make a list for you and you take part in the fun, too. It is important for them to see you having fun as well.
- Running can be a team sport. Rope in as many friends as possible.
- Run to a destination. Run to the park where you will have a picnic and catch the bus home or get picked up. Or do it the other way around and get dropped off somewhere and you

have to run home. This in many ways sets up the feeling that running can take you places – literally. It avoids the feeling that running is just training. Run around a park and you end up where you started, just more tired. Running and ending up somewhere different gives you a sense of achievement, awareness of distance and the seed is planted that you can start running a bit further than you thought!

- Visit a different place and run. Running is a great way to explore a new place.

30 Beach fun

A Year Outside Challenge
19 December
Weather: Cold, drizzly

I guess none of us are convinced, given the weather, but Duncan insists that the beach will be a nice change to our usual mountain walk. We rather reluctantly join him for the half-hour car journey, but when we get there everyone seems a little more keen to get out and about and a little happier too. We walk up and down, then find a rather sheltered part next to some rocks, and the boys start playing in the sand, safely away from the chilly waves. The light drizzle has given the sand enough moisture to retain its shape, and so they start building castles, digging moats and decorating with various sticks and pebbles. A.B.

In the first part of the book, on the benefits of outdoors, I mention a study aptly named 'Happiness is greater in natural environments'[1] which used smartphone data to precisely locate where we are when we are happiest. One of the results of the study, aside from what the title obviously suggests, is also the association between coastal and marine environments with subjective well-being, i.e. happiness. In other words, being by the sea seems to make us happier.

The authors of the study characteristically write, in an effort to explain the magnitude of the effect: 'Marine and coastal margins are by some distance the happiest locations, with responses approximately 6 points higher than continuous urban environments on the 0–100 scale. Alternatively expressed, [. . .] the difference between attending an exhibition and doing housework.'

How lucky then, that if you live in the UK you are very likely to be only a daytrip away from the nearest beach (Coton in the Elms, Derbyshire, is officially the furthest point from the sea, at a distance of seventy miles). And although most of us associate the beach with summertime, there are several activities that are not restricted to fair weather days. As long as it's not too windy, the beach can be enjoyed year round.

1 MacKerron, G., & Mourato, S. (2013). Happiness is greater in natural environments. *Global Environmental Change, 23*(5), 992–1000.

TAKING IT FURTHER

- **Beach art** If you are lucky enough to have access to a sandy beach, take advantage with a host of sand-building activities. From the classic sandcastle, to a sandman (the beach alternative to the classic snowman) and from the simple but labour intensive tunnel to the sea, to the sand city, sand, combined with water, offers the perfect medium for a variety of creations. Offer children open-ended tasks and watch them let their imagination run wild. Decorate your sculptures with bits of driftwood, rocks and pebbles or any other natural materials that are at hand. Don't forget to take a picture!
- **Beachcombing** The simple activity of walking by the tideline and looking for items the sea has washed up can offer hours of fun. Look for shells, sticks and stones and make a collection. Depending on the time of year, tide and recent weather events, like storms, different kinds of objects will wash up. NB: make sure to leave your sea shells behind (see page 143).
- **Sand writing and drawing** Practise your writing or drawing skills in the sand. Play noughts and crosses, which although a simple game, has great pedagogical value, teaching kids to take turns, and good sportsmanship. For older children a game of improvised pictionary can be a lot of fun too.

Endnote

This book, as well as my family's experience in our year spent outdoors, is a mere introduction to what I hope will be a lifelong relationship. A first date, of sorts, to a long-lasting partner in life and a relationship that will evolve, change and deepen as our children grow. My hope is that this book will provide you with ideas for making the introduction between your child and the natural world around us. Starting from a place of pure fun and exploration, children can then build their own special relationship with the outdoors, connecting and engaging with nature in ways that they choose.

Duncan and I are lucky to be in touch with a lot of our ex-pupils and have seen first hand the benefits of encouraging children to get to know, and feel at home in, the outdoors. Many of them, now in their early to mid-teens, some older, actively choose to spend time in nature – exploring their limits, finding entertainment and excitement, but also a shelter from the demands of adolescence and early adulthood.

We both sincerely hope that you have enjoyed trying at least a few of these activities and that you have been inspired also to let your children guide you towards other possibilities, that echo their own interests and capture their imagination. Finally, we hope that you will see the benefits that we have seen in our own children, and the children we teach – the benefits of growing up wild and in touch with nature. See you out there!

Alexia and Duncan Barrable

APPENDIX

Designing an outdoor play area

Designing an outdoor play space at home should provide your children with hours of learning and fun all year round. A space for children needs to be just that – for children. Often areas are designed with an adult's thinking of what children should be getting up to, or worse, for it to be in keeping with the garden. Of course no one wants it to look like a hurricane has blown through that corner of the yard. You will have to give up a little feng shui for the greater good if you want your children to be engaged, to have the freedom to experiment and like it or not take the odd risk or two in what they are doing. How often have you bought a toy or activity and found that your child prefers to use it quite differently from its intended purpose? Setting aside a space for your child to play and learn can be done successfully even in the smallest of gardens.

ELEMENTS TO INCLUDE IN YOUR DESIGN

Designing the perfect play area is not something we are going to tell you how to do as everyone's available space and resources differ. But what we will do is cover the elements that have been shown to work in being best able to engage children as well as to assist in their play to promote early developmental skills. In an interesting five-year study in Vancouver which observed children's behaviours, it has been found to the chagrin of several local authorities that costly traditionally built community playgrounds dominated by equipment failed to entice children and were not being used the way they were designed.[1] Creating a space that incorporates your child's interests and allows them to exert a measure of control of it, for example being able to rearrange objects like tables, chairs or logs is one of the most vital elements when considering your design. When you are able to observe how children play, or take part in child-led play you are given an important glimpse into a child's world.[2] Here are a few elements that you can incorporate when designing your own:

- ***Plan for year round use, sun and rain shelters***
  Just because it isn't a warm July day doesn't mean the play area shouldn't be used. With careful thought it can be used all year round, allowing children to enjoy the opportunities that the seasons provide such as ice sculpting, collecting autumn leaves, and if there is a sheltered area outdoor playtime is extended.

1 https://www.evergreen.ca/downloads/pdfs/Landscape-Child-Development.pdf

2 Blasi, M. & Hurwitz, S. C. (2002). For Parents Particularly: To Be Successful – Let Them Play! *Childhood education*, *79*(2), 101–2.

- ***Multi-purpose elements***

  Logs, stones: these allow for change and evolution. Screens and potted plants can all have different uses and can be made to suit various play activities.

- ***Loose parts***

  These can be all manner of things. Old tupperware, kitchen spatulas and wooden spoons, child-sized furnishings, bowls, containers, gardening tools, funnels, magnifying lenses, even a section of garden hose. It is the little things like these that children can rearrange and use their imagination with.

- ***Hiding and shelters***

  A kitchen, a house, a den or a fort are all places that children like to imagine themselves in. Even if the fort consists of a large shrub and some chairs. Children need a place to retreat, hide and tell stories, secrets even! That is not to say they should be out of sight – a trellis, shrubbery, some poles sunk into the ground that a sheet can be tied to are all simple ways to provide a place of refuge for your child's imagination to run wild.

- ***Physical development, risk and challenge***

  Children need to push, pull, dig, lift, jump and climb. Allowing for children to take risks safely allows them to test and explore their capabilities. Swings, ropes, logs to balance on are all part of letting them learn. From a young age, play is used to test limits and to repeat skills until they have mastered them.[1] Restrictions on risky outdoor play, it has been suggested, can actually hinder development.[2]

- ***Let nature in***

  Providing naturals elements in a play space is very important. From trees, bushes, long grass, rocks, potted plants, to a vegetable patch, snails, even a home (if you are comfortable with this) for solitary bees. All provide a tactile and sensory link with nature.

- ***Let your space evolve***

  The seasons change, interests grow and wane and sadly children grow up all too fast. Be open to a request that *Princess Margo's Mud Pie Shoppe* needs to make way for a small climbing wall, or that a pirate's rope ladder be installed where her vegetable garden once grew.

OPPORTUNITIES FOR PRACTISING SKILLS

Not only is there a consistent positive relationship between outdoor time and physical activity for both boys and girls,[3] but a

1 Play England, http://www.playengland.org.uk/media/70684/design-for-play.pdf accessed 6 August 2016

2 Brussoni, M., Olsen, L. L., Pike, I., & Sleet, D. A. (2012). Risky play and children's safety: Balancing priorities for optimal child development. *International journal of environmental research and public health*, 9(9), 3134–48.

3 Gray, C., Gibbons, R., Larouche, R., Sandseter, E. B. H., Bienenstock, A., Brussoni, M., . . . & Power, M. (2015). What is the relationship between

child's imagination, dexterity, emotional and physical strength can all be developed through creative play.[1] Freedom to play, to manipulate objects and to experiment all allow for children to practise decision making, engage fully in their activities and has shown to improve their learning too.[2]

For each of the skills there are links to activities in this book:

Fine motor skills

Sand play (p. 76)

Mud play (p. 144)

Water play (p. 103)

Leaf art (p. 135)

Gross motor skills

Sand play (p. 76)

Climbing (p. 148)

Climbing and balancing (p. 148)

outdoor time and physical activity, sedentary behaviour, and physical fitness in children? A systematic review. *International journal of environmental research and public health*, *12*(6), 6455–74.

1 Ginsburg, K. R. (2007). The importance of play in promoting healthy child development and maintaining strong parent-child bonds. *Pediatrics,119*(1), 182–91.

2 Sobel, D. M., & Kushnir, T. (2003). Interventions do not solely benefit causal learning: Being told what to do results in worse learning than doing it yourself. In *Proceedings of the twenty-fifth annual meeting of the Cognitive Science Society*.

Independence

Running (p. 152)

Scavenger hunts (p. 106)

The elements

Boat races (p. 52)

Rainy day fun (p. 142)

Let's go fly a kite (p. 109)

Creativity and problem solving

Fewer things, more play (p. 79)

Wild food (p. 131)

Sand play (p. 76)

Water play (p. 103)

Risk

Character building (benefits) (p. 27)

The forgotten art of tree climbing (p. 148)

Index

Growing Up Happy: Ten proven ways to increase your child's happiness and well-being

Alexia Barrable and Dr Jenny Barnett

Available to buy in ebook and paperback

A guide to nurturing positive habits and happiness skills that will last a lifetime.

In *Growing Up Happy*, neuroscientist Dr Jenny Barnett, and teacher and mum Alexia Barrable describe scientifically-proven methods by which children's happiness can be boosted in just a few minutes each day.

With easy-to-use activities for toddlers through to teenagers, this book steers the reader through simple and practical ways, grounded in scientific research, to enhance children's – and adults' – day-to-day happiness.

Stress-Free Feeding: How to develop healthy eating habits in your child

Lucy Cooke and Laura Webber

Available to buy in ebook and paperback

A practical guide to feeding problems in children from 0 to 5, and how to solve them.

Using case studies and real-life examples, this book is full of sound expert advice on how best to feed your young children. It helps you understand the science, dispel the myths and see that other parents have similar concerns.

With hints and tips for each stage of feeding that will help develop healthy eating patterns for life, this book will put the pleasure back into family mealtimes.

Mum's Sneaky Recipes

Samantha Quinn

Coming soon in ebook and paperback

Has your dining room turned into a battleground when it comes to mealtimes? Do your children's fussy eating habits regularly negate your efforts to offer healthier meals? If the answer to either of these questions is 'yes', Mum's Sneaky Recipes can help.

Mum's Sneaky Recipes will help you gently and lovingly redirect your kids towards nutritious meals and snacks, rebalance your whole family's eating routines and improve their overall health and wellbeing.

[illegible]

[illegible]

[illegible]

[illegible]

[illegible]

[illegible]

[illegible]

How to Raise a [illegible]